Muse Power

How Recreational Music Making
Heals Us from Depression
and Other Symptoms
of Modern Culture

Cheri Shanti

PUBLISHED BY G.L.DESIGN, BOULDER, CO

Muse Power:
How Recreational Music Making Heals Us from Depression
and Other Symptoms of Modern Culture
1st Edition

Library of Congress Control Number: 2008936569
ISBN10: 1-933983-08-6
ISBN13: 978-1-933983-08-0

PUBLISHED BY G.L.DESIGN
2090 GRAPE AVE
BOULDER, CO 80304

Invitation

If you've ever felt alone in this world
Disconnected, pushed out, stepped on
by the Machine of Modern Madness

If you've ever walked thru the world like a shadow
Melancholy and curiously confused
Looking for some deeper way to connect
Looking in every pair of eyes for something shared

If you've ever felt the loss of tribe and community
The isolation of living in boxes far from family or friends
If you've ever cried at night
Yearning for others who understand
Craving something deeper

Then I invite you to the Worlds of the Muse
I invite you to step into the joy of music making
Wholeheartedly
And let your heart be opened to it's power
To heal, to transform, to reconnect

Right Now at this very moment
There are people dancing, singing and sharing
Somewhere in the World
There is always music happening
The Muses wait for us to play with them
They are always there waiting for a chance to dance thru us

Music heals us
Music brings us together
Music builds community
Music is the universal language of all time, all space

This is your invitation!
It is always open to you!

DEDICATION & THANKS

I dedicate this book to those all over the world who know the power in unity and in empowering each other to fully express themselves in community thru music and love.

I offer it to those who are alone, lost in depression, anxiety or overwhelm who are so in need of supportive ways to bring the joy back into their lives. I offer it to the dancer, the singer, the poet, the musician in each and everyone of us living on planet earth.

And to all those who have shared the joy of all night music making with me and seen the pure light of God shining thru the eyes of everyone there as the sun reminds us of our true essence.

I offer it to my family who doesn't understand why this magic of music has taken my life in such a "weird" direction, that someday they too will be in circle with me, seeing and feeling the joy of sharing ourselves together in the Muse.

This sharing is for the Muse that lives inside each one of us in unique ways. It is really a socio-musicological perspective of something we all can feel easily in our hearts that no words can truly express fully.

And specifically, I give great gratitude to:
    *the Creator of Life for this opportunity to dance in flesh on
      the Earth
    *my parents, Lois & Barry Lunn, for their teachings and
      bringing me into this earthly realm
    *my good friends Amy Miller & Morgan Ryan for gifting
      me the opportunity to be warm while focusing my time and
      energy on this project
    *my beloved, Jessee Layton, who has afforded me the luxury
      of time to write and create while knowing I had a home
      to come back to, and who has supported me in coming fully
      back to my passion thru music & drumming
    *my students and friends who inspire and encourage me
    *my mentors and co-creators of this movement:
      Jeff Magnus McBride, Abigal Spinner, Adam Fleisher,
      the whole Santa Cruz Firedance community, Graywolf, Paul

Temple, Royel Wooten and all those who have shared fire light with me.

Most of all, I give thanks to the Ultimate spirit of LOVE, God, the Great Spirit, whatever you want to call it, the power which creates and sustains life, which has guided me to this path and been my deepest teacher and my steadfest, loyal friend and companion thru countless hours of observation of myself, the dancers, and the power of rhythm to melt all illusion. My truest and best friend since before the beginning of time. In humble love and devotion, I offer thanks.

AUTHOR'S NOTE

It is important for me to be clear that I do not, in any way, claim to be an expert on any particular form of traditional drum and dance culture, music or musicology. My interest has always been rooted in personal expression, creativity and the creation of something as yet unformed; something that lies in our future more than our past. My astrologer has told me that I am one who bridges the ancient with the future or the not yet present, and I feel that truth in many ways in my life, especially in music.I know that the ancient cultures and traditions have much to teach us, and I also Feel strongly that there is a call to create something that works for our culture in it's present form in this whacky, western, modern world. My interest lies in discovering where we, as westerners, are now, what may have contributed to getting us here, and how to move from this place into a deeper understanding of ourselves thru music, expression and community. I have taken the time to learn rhythmical foundations, basic skills, fundamentals of etiquette, technique and expression, and have applied those basic principles to the work I do now with drum, dance, and transformational alchemy thru community music. I proclaim to be nothing more than myself and know there is much to learn. I realize fully that there will be many facets that are not touched on in this book!

The intention of writing this is threefold: one is simply to share my experiences and the experiences of others in relation to the mysterious openings and transformations that are possible through drumming, dancing and rhythmical expressions. Another is to explore the deep call that we all have to be together in ways that modern culture doesn't really seem to provide space for. The third is to offer insight into how to overcome our fears and the "I can't do it" programming around the sacred and magical play of music making in all it's forms and to bring it into our lives as a daily practice.

The stories shared throughout this book and in Chapter 9 are from everyday people, some are "musicians" and most are not. Most are average people who would not consider themselves "musicians" in the formal sense of the word, they don't study chords, theory or practice an instrument. Their experiences will show what possibilities exist for transformation, human connection and community in very real ways thru the eyes of real, everday, common people. These beings have experienced a greater sense of community, a deeper feeling of "belonging," and an ability to overcome depression, anxiety and deep seated fears thru the experiences of playing music, dancing, drumming and participatory music making.

I hope to inspire more community sharing in each reader, thru music making, drumming, and dancing together. It is my experience that being together in these ancient and familiar ways strengthens a community and the individuals in it in ways that are indescribable but very real. It has transformed my life deeply to participate, witness and observe the subtle and powerful ways that music can work thru us.

I sincerely hope that this book touches something in you and entices you to play, dance, sing and share more with others thru the Magic and Mystery of the Muse within you!

PREFACE

Cheri Shanti's musical path and mine have followed some very similar trajectories. I was very honored when she requested that I write this preface. My evolution as community musician has culminated in the creation of a non-profit organization called Musical Missions of Peace which raises funds to carry community music-making into international arenas. My non-profit organization has recently helped fund an American woman to travel through Iran, sowing the seeds of connection and friendship by joining in village festivals across the Persian countryside.

Musical Missions of Peace also currently supports music lessons for Iraqi refugee children which in Syria and in Jordan. These schools provide employment for displaced professional Iraqi musicians and help ensure that the valuable content of ancient Iraqi musical tradition is not lost during these times of upheaval.

My community music engagements have ranged from Native American festivals in Peru and Mexico, to Greece and finally, during recent years, to Egypt, Syria, Iraq, Jordan, Palestine and Lebanon.

My years of study of the ancient micro-tonal music scales and the music of the Arab world have enabled me to feel a sense of belonging in many far-flung community settings in the Middle East. Ah, if only the politicians could experience some of these same things!

Early in life I spent years in counter-cultural communes across the Western states in the USA and I led many live music events when it was time to celebrate.

I have had the great pleasure to join with Cheri in some of her Colorado-based community "Muse" and "Fire Ceremony" celebrations and have been delighted to feel the powerful energy and clarity of vision which she brings to each occasion.

Baghdad, Iraq: Unified by a favorite old Iraqi song we stand and move our bodies together while the high-rise buildings burn and the invading army tanks drive by. Musical reality is more cohesive than military reality. This is what I have discovered. When will the soldiers lay down their guns and pick up the flutes and the lutes and the tambourines? The ancient wisdom tells us that this option does exist! It works for us here on the streets of Baghdad: we are American citizens singing with Iraqis here in the ancient Iraqi capitol even as we all mourn the destruction.

In this book, Cheri reveals her experiences drumming with women in India and we discover that there are indeed other tools for cross-cultural commuication which, unfortunately, are generally omitted from US foreign policy around the globe. Connecting through the universal language of music offers us familiar and respectful ways to bridge worlds.

Sina, Peru: Tucked into a village in a valley high on the slopes of the Andes above the Amazon jungle the Inca-speaking families are into the third night of the celebration. Clapping their hands for rhythm in their dance they sing of the loneliness of the vast mountain landscapes. They sing of the pain of lost loves and of the hopes for new romance. Eusevio Qispi has planted the cornerstone for his new house! Tears come as he sings in anticipation of the arrival of his new bride! No one mentions the one awkward detail: he has yet to succeed with romance and the bride is entirely imaginary. But never mind! Four days and nights of singing and clapping the village rhythms will surely help to conjure her up!

Cheri's elucidations of the roles music plays in tribal societies around the world make it clear that brides can indeed miraculously appear when the right music is played long and sincerely enough!

West Bank of the Nile, Egypt: The piercing wails of three ancient oboes ride atop the skilled drum-strokes on the skin of the big bass drum. Dressed in their white robes the village men whirl at opposite ends of their ceremonial dancing sticks. The flavor of a martial art stylizes the dance. There are no gaps in the music between midnight and dawn. Once again all turmoils and struggles have been laid to rest for an entire night. From time to time a woman dances solo in the center of the courtyard beneath the appreciative gaze of the assembled men. All is just as it should be. The atmosphere is absolutely Egyptian! Eight thousand years of ancestral rhythmic tradition manifests once again and carries our energy up into the sky!

In this book we discover that Cheri has been laying the same foundations for rhythmic tradition right here in the USA! Her work offers a place for us here in the US to find this kind of experience, a place to lay down the struggles and turmoils of the world and be together, in spite of our differences, and celebrate life in community.

Naxos, Greece: Tonight the island drummers and musicians have congregated in a small town near the northernmost Mediterranean beach. While the lines of dancers revolve under the moon a wave of energy carries the energy to new highs: the rhythm has suddenly shifted from seven-beat phrases to eight-beat phrases! Without a single break the band plays until past dawn. Dancing all night is something taken for granted as a natural human right!

Cheri's clear statements about the strangeness of some of the still existing rules about MUSIC "disturbing the peace" here in our homeland can help us bring about changes in values. There are few cultures in the world where music making on a community level are so restricted, repressed and devalued as it is in the US. The freedom to gather and play music, anytime, anywhere is not something we are familiar with in the US.

Sinaloa, Mexico: It's now four o'clock in the morning in a small mountain town. A group of fifteen guitar players serenade the crowd from the front porches of randomly chosen homes along the neighborhood streets. The highly amplified dance band in the central plaza has finished for the night. Now there is acoustic space for random improvisation! This village has truly come alive!

Here, as in most of the indigenously intact cultures in the more tropical parts of the world, the music is "by, for and of" all the age groups in the community: the children, the teenagers, the adults and the grandparents. In this book you will find beautiful descriptions which hint at the beauty of this reality, although, as one of her quoted contributors mentions, you really had to be there!

Deep in the Grand Canyon: The rhythm fever is upon us! Anything will do: we extract whatever pots and pans and jars and cans we can find from the cooking gear on our tethered rafts. Spoons make great drum sticks! Which parts of our primal identities will emerge during the next few hours of frenzied playing? High moonlit rocky crags stand sentinel for the duration of the night. Musical moments are punctuated with the sights and sounds of ecstatic human bodies diving into the fast-moving river waters of the Colorado. Everyone swims back for more. The next day there is a special satisfaction in the air.

In her chapter on the glamorization of popular music, Cheri gives our young folks some encouragement for personal participation in the communal creation of rhythm and music even as we observe the trends toward electronica.

Amman, Jordan: Thirty Iraqi refugees gather in a friend's apartment. Dinner is shared but then the drums and instruments come out of their cases. As the rhythms bubble out of their fingers onto their drums, the refugees burning questions around basic survival gradually recede from the forefront of consiousness. Someone has begun to sing. An ancient stringed instrument, the Arabic lute, is in the hands of a skilled player. Drums begin the accompaniment. A violin appears. Five hours later the dancing and singing are still in full swing. Spoken words and conversation will have to wait for another time. Now we are in a space made sacred by the rhythms of the ancient muses of the Mesopotamian Tigris and Euphrates river people!

What are the glues and fabrics of cultural identity which can hold people together even in extreme times of disruption and catastrophe? Cheri examines the trends in music teaching in American schools and makes some clear-cut suggestions.

Boulder, Colorado: Seventy-five dancers reach the stage of screaming and singing out their ecstasy. Four percussionists are here in the ballroom well into the second hour of rhythmic ebb and flow. The sound is live and no amplification is needed. The drummers and the dancers adjust the tempo and no electronic tracks are included. A wave of refreshment rolls through our consciousness as we celebrate our freedom from the usual electronica. Cheri Shanti is one of the drummers.

What do all these scenes have in common? Music is flowing. Love is flowing. Bonding is happening. No one is divided. No one is separate or left out! No one has reason for plotting or trickery. We are all one. Even aging bodies feel pain-free and young again! The elixir of communal music is being served by these drummers and musicians who have evolved to become the local shamans and priestesses. The ancestors are having their say and harmony has been achieved. What a magnificent model for the rest of life!

This book is about the positive chemical makeup of community musical gatherings and the healthy resonances which they predictably generate.

Cameron Powers

TABLE OF CONTENTS

Introduction

The night is cold and dark. A full moon hangs low on the horizon: orange, bright and promising of some other worldly magic. The sound of drums, rattles, bells, and voices intermingle, creating a wild cacophony of sound that reverberates for miles in every direction. Around a blazing fire, bodies move, circling in both directions: feet pounding the earth in rhythm to the drummer's songs, arms and bodies moving as if by some other will than just the dancer's own. Some of the dancers have rattles, some have bells around their ankles, some are arm in arm moving around the fire in council. Some have painted faces, some are adorned with feathers, and bones, others are all in white, some are naked or half naked. Around the edges of the circle, people of all ages mingle; talking, laughing, sharing food and moving about in many forms of prayerful offerings.

The drums get louder, faster and more intense and suddenly a woman breaks into song as if on cue. Her voice wild, free, and beautifully human, wails over even the loudest drum. The song is telling a story: a story of pain, of human endurance and a greater truth. The song touches another dancer who responds in a rhythmic chant, and then another, and within minutes all of the dancers are singing, creating layer upon layer of sound and expression. Slowly the drummers soften, and the voices are carrying a new song into the night. A soft cloud emerges over the moon, darkening the sky. The fire softens and only the voices are heard. The rhythm is carried on by the bare feet of the dancers.

Looking at this gathering from the outside, deep in the heart of the woods, fire blazing, drums resounding, spirit songs emerging from wailing hearts, it might be hard to tell when or where in time you are. The familiarity of it is inexplicable yet profound; primal and somehow undeniably intriguing. It could be in Africa somewhere, or a ceremony in North America before the Europeans came, or it could be a modern tribe somewhere in the United States, which indeed it is.

Out of this space, one young woman steps forward into the center of the circle, close to the fire. She is in her early 20's and she is flanked by two other women who are holding space for her, energetically supporting her. She is silently acknowledged by all present and begins to speak. The singing voices continue on, but intuitively all the singers bring the volume down so that this young woman's voice can be heard clearly.

"I come before you tonight," says the young woman, dressed all in white with her head held high, "to tell a story of a girl I knew. She was lost in this world. She felt no connection to her family, or to the kids at school. She felt life had no purpose as everything she saw around her seemed to only offer hope of an even more isolated existence, to become yet another cog in the wheel of the machine. In her confusion, in her loneliness and despair, she became depressed and angry at the world for being so screwed up, for offering so little that has substance. Kids at school were doing drugs, heroine, coke, pills, pot, and she wanted to fit in. It seemed like a place she could escape reality at least. That was how she became a heroin addict, 5 years ago."

By now, the voices are the softest echo, but still there, energetically supporting this young woman fully, empowering her to continue. "Tonight, I am here to ask you, my community, to bear witness to this story. That girl was me. I was a heroin addict, and tonight I am committing to her, and to you, who love me and hear me now, that I am finished with that addiction, and I am choosing life. With you as my witness, and with your love and support, I honor my past and give thanks for the lessons I have learned. Thank you for hearing me tonight." She threw a wrapped object into the fire, no one asked what it was. The voices fell silent and 250 people stood in total support and awe at this young woman's testimony, by firelight and moonlight. The dancers kept pace around the fire in the silence, and the cloud moved across the moon allowing it to beam it's full radiance on the face of this young woman who had just stepped forth to bare her soul. She was truly beautiful, radiant and angelic by moonlight.

After a few moments of silence, a man's voice emerged, softly and with profound tenderness singing, "You are my family and you are healing me," and the rest of the group instantly chimed in, "I am your family and I am healing you, together we are one, we are one." The drums slowly began and merged with the voices, and the woman danced a solo dance around the fire with tears streaming down her face. She looked pure, and angelic in white with her newly shorn bald head bobbing slowly in tempo. Looking around the circle, I saw that many people were wiping tears, hugging each other and feeling the joy that was emerging and rippling thru this tender moment. The rest of this night, all the way until dawn, held a deep grace that will never be forgotten by those present.

This is a true story, and one of the many powerful experiences I've ever witnessed in a circle. To see how her sharing effected the entire night, and each individual present there, and to see how empowered and strong she felt that she could come forth like this, in front of 250 people, many of whom she didn't know. I knew this young woman. She was very shy, she usually barely spoke a word. Yet she felt safe enough, supported enough, in this circle to come forth and to literally unveil her deepest pain and shame and allow it to be transformed!

I've had so many amazing experiences thru the expressive arts community sharing, but this one was beyond words to witness. This woman's fearlessness, transparency and the total and complete compassion, grace and sweetness that she was held in during and after her sharing was truly one of the most graceful and transcendent experiences of my life.

The Drummer's Path: A Doorway to Myself and Community

People often ask me how I started drumming, or how I "found" the drum, and I always say that the drum found me. I wasn't looking to start drumming, nor did I even know, at that time, that there was a world of drumming outside of what I'd seen at shows and concerts. I definitely always had an attraction to rhythm and dance, but to play a drum wasn't something I had ever envisioned before it happened. I had just never been exposed to it, coming from a fairly conservative background in Florida.

My first drum experience occurred when I was in college in Boulder, CO. I had just gone to a barn party in Nederland, Colorado where Leftover Salmon was playing. That was back in the days when they were still playing barn parties, before they got big. After the show there was a party that I went to with a friend to unwind before driving down the canyon. When I got there, in the loft upstairs, there were a bunch of guys playing drums. I'd never heard anything like it, and was open enough to feel a bit wild and crazy and something clicked in me, "I can do that! I want to do that!" I asked permission to play, and closed my eyes and just played what came, I had no idea if I was doing something right or wrong, and in all honesty, it wasn't even a consideration in my mind. I was simply feeling and playing. As a dancer, I knew rhythm very well, and I just put my feet in my hands!

I don't know how long we played, but somehow we had one of those magical moments of all stopping together on the same beat, and all of those guys were just staring at me with their jaws dropped. Suddenly I knew I must have done something awfully wrong! One of the guys finally asked, "How long have you been playing?"

"I don't know, 10 minutes? How long have we been playing?"

And all of them started patting me on the back and high fiving me, "You rock,"
"You're amazing,"
"No way, No way." Apparently, I had played so well that none of them could believe it was the first time I'd touched a drum. The journey had begun and the next day I found myself buying my first set of congas.

The Drummer's path for me has expanded far beyond the drum, into a Spiritual and Musical Ministry of Transformation, Alchemy and Creative Self Expression. It has become a life study of relationship with self and others, and of community, of healing, and of a process of Evolution of the soul and personality. My friend Royel Wooten, (Futureman) uses the term "Evolution d'amour" in his work and I completely resonate with that on my journey. It has been a learning to love, honor and respect self, and others. In all honestly, it is less about the rhythms and the technical aspects of drumming for me, and more about how we relate to each other, and how vibrations affect individuals, groups and dynamics. It is about how individuals in a group can work together to create harmonious interplay that is natural, spontaneous and authentic while also allowing and supporting full individual expression. It is about how I can get out of the way to let the greater work come thru and be present. In the past few years I've realized I can do my work just as effectively in groups by not playing as I can by playing, in fact usually more effectively!

One of my first teachers, Michael Moses Tirsch, said to me one night shortly after he'd first seen me play, "If you take this path, know that it will reveal everything about yourself to you." At the time I sort of shrugged it off; years later I called him to acknowledge that indeed the path was showing me far more than I maybe even wanted to see at that time. Now, I feel so blessed for the wisdom and the humility this path has offered me and will continue to gift me in future evolutions.

My personal path with the drum has shown me, over and over, that the drum is a tool to access something that is more universal than any one culture or tradition. I am not a traditional drummer by any means. I have studied the basic fundamentals of African, Afro-Cuban, Mid-Eastern and other traditions and very much value the traditional cultures, and respect them deeply. It just hasn't been my primary focus. I feel that there is something equally valid that is being birthed in finding our own pulse, rhythms and expressions and my passion has been for exploring what lies inside of us that is authentically our own cultural expression thru the drum, and music. There is so much to learn from these traditions, and it is easy to spend a lifetime studying just one and still just barely scratch the surface of the wisdom therein. Some of the experiences I've had with traditional rhythm, songs, and Deities, have convinced me fully that they are not something to take lightly, that they do indeed invoke energies and forces that are deep, ancient and very alive, and that a little bit of knowledge without discernment or full initiation/education can lead to a potentially dangerous situation, as those ancient rhythms do truly invoke Spirits and powers of the Other worlds.

There was a night at a drum circle at a festival in North Carolina. The fire was raging, and the pit was full of young, wild drummers, as well as a few skilled players who were performing (as was I) at the festival. The rain started. Really it was a storm, full on with thunder and lightning. A man I knew from other circles started to scream at the top of his lungs to Chango, the Santeria God of Thunder and Lightning. I saw that he was trying to force a rhythm onto the circle which was quite unnatural and since I could see that Chango was already quite present and possibly agitated, I got one of those intuitive hits to move on and began to pack up my gear. Just as I got my drum packed and turned to go, I heard a crack, and turned to see a tree fall smack on this man's drum, also cracking down pretty hard on his shoulder. It broke his drum, obviously, and quieted him down pretty quickly. Certainly one of the most memorable experiences of seeing the direct response of a deity who apparently didn't appreciate the manner in which he was yelled at, and an experience none present are likely to forget. His arm was in a sling for several weeks after that and he didn't drum for almost 2 months.

I honor the traditional cultures and their vast wisdom and understanding of rhythm, music and the divine connection, and I respect those who spend their lives learning these ways and studying them. What I am more interested in, however, is what is coming thru us now as beings living in the modern world. What is emerging thru us as westerners without any real rhythm tradition, per se, behind us to learn from, or be born into? What is our unique and authentic connection?

I feel that every place on the planet has it's own rhythm, it's own "feel" or "vibration" and that there is a deep universal pulse that runs through all of it. African music is unlike music from any other part of the world, it's complexity and richness and feel is inherently African. People born into it have a natural connection to that music and indeed it has influenced much of the world's music today. Irish and Celtic music holds a totally different vibration, Native Americans' music is unique to the people and places and has a consistent feeling that represents their land and ways. If we only copy and imitate these other traditions, it is my personal feeling that we are missing something of our own authenticity.

Daniel Levitin in "This is your Brain on Music" writes that our brains and the music we use culturally co-evolve, or develop together, and that young children will begin showing a preference for the music of their own culture by age two. (p. 229) Levitin writes that researchers have also found that babies can hear music in the womb, and that they will recognize and actually prefer music played to them in utero after they are born. The auditory system of a fetus is fully functional as early as 20 weeks after conception! (p. 223) Our relationship to music is very influenced, though certainly not fully determined, by our culture and what we were exposed to, both in the womb and during the first few years of development.

As Westerners, we simply have a different relationship to rhythm than Africa or Egypt or Morocco. We can try to play their music, even get really good at it, learn their songs in their languages, dance their dances, but what of our own as a culture? My curiosity lies in exploring that and finding our own identity as a rhythm-culture in formation in the modern, western culture. Being that there is such a blend of ethnicities, music and world influence here, naturally it will be some kind of a blend of the world's voices, but to try to take on and copy another culture's music totally, just doesn't feel authentic for me personally and so I don't base my work in that arena. I do honor those who do and realize that Westerners who are learning the music of traditional cultures are playing a big role in helping to preserve that music and keep it alive. That is a great and worthy endeavor! And the discipline it takes to learn these forms is profound!

This book is an exploration of music and the human connection and on how it can help us now, in the modern world, to re-connect to each other by learning how to work and play together in community. While a lot of my personal experience and stories will relate to the Drum and dance culture specifically, I will also be exploring folk music, the glamorization of music, modern "trance" DJ dances, and other forms of creative participatory expression in this book as pathways for Personal transformation, community building and self reflection. I subscribe to the more traditional/tribal way of viewing music, in that I include dance, song, instruments, melody, rhythm and all aspects of the muse in my working definition of music. I see them as inseparable parts of a whole, so when I say "muse" or "music" in this book, I am referring to all of these forms.

There are many avenues to explore in the arena of Personal Transformation and Development, and all are powerful portals to opening the doors to understanding ourselves and the world we live in. The expressive musical arts path is unique, for me, in that it is a path we can explore both individually and together as a community or group. Often we can do this simultaneously, meaning we can be having a deep personal individual experience in the midst of a group and be witnessed and witnessing others in that space also. It fosters great reflection and transparency and invites a deep and authentic sharing. It allows for total spontaneity, form and function without closing any part of the whole off or denying any part of ourselves. It supports and strongly requests that we bring ALL of ourselves to the experience. In doing that, we not only show up and feel our own connection, but we inspire and give the freedom for others to step up and into their expression too. Drum and dance and community music making in particular holds something deep, primal and tribal that brings us back into connection with the Earth, and with ancestors that we may or may not share blood with, but whose land we walk on every day. It unifies us with an ancient connection while providing us with context for today's world. It calls on the deepest cellular memories of our being-ness to remember who we are, where we come from and our ancestors. It requests from us that we consider where we want to go as humans sharing the planet and how we want to interact on our journey to get there.

It is my prayer that the sharing offered here, in this book, will hold examples of what is possible for us as individuals and as a greater community of beings who are committed to learning the arts of relationship, working and playing together, with conscious awareness and mutual support. It is my intention also that this book will inspire people to create opportunities to practice the Sacred Art of playing music as part of community building and re-localization efforts.

I believe that "those who play together, stay together," and that as the stresses of the modern world continue to build, making music together is one way that we can continue to evolve and participate in the process of global transformation on both community and individual levels.

Recreational Music Making
Community Music Defined

For the purposes of this book, for the most part, when I refer to "Community Music" or "Music Making" I am referring to music that is in the moment, spontaneous and a group experience that is very much in alignment with a term that the American Music Conference (AMC) termed "Recreational Music making" (RMM). In essence, the heart of RMM is that it removes the concept that music is only for musicians who have spent their lives studying theory and practicing every day. It in no way de-values that, and instead simply asserts that making music belongs to everyone. It can take the form of just messing around with your friends, or it can be more organized, like the drum circles that many employers, health care facilities, schools and groups are turning to as team-building and community building exercises.

Chapter 1

Symptoms
of a
Lost Connection

"What a grip this techno world has on me... and I don't even want it! I seem to think I should know better, but I am doing it, looking always for that next fix. Everything in between is full of an absence of connection to life. Sometimes I think maybe I am swimming in this silly world just to get a feel for the milieu, so that I can help rescue others later. It's creepy, and it is very real   ."
Christina Bertelli, Boulder, CO

"I feel disconnected from community, isolated, lost, lonely, confused, overwhelmed. Have felt disconnected here for 18 years, but things like work, caring for elderly parents, take my mind off of it. It usually comes back to feeling isolated."
Anonymous Email

"How to live in this world but not of it now... I do hope I can get a handle on it myself soon. Because this world and it's ways has tired me really. Everything seems to be just a band-aid sometimes. I imagine myself heading for the hills more frequently. This tangled web I find myself in seems to get tighter and appears to lead to a more neurotic type of society."
Jenny Sustello

The modern world we live in is a fascinating and mysterious place. We can travel to and communicate from the most remote parts of the globe in less time than it once took to go a hundred miles. We can cook food in under a minute, when it once took maybe an hour or more to make the fire, boil water, and cook it. Our bodies get propelled thru space in vehicles that offer the convience of going farther and faster than our ancestors ever dreamed possible. The wisdom and knowledge of the entire world is now at our fingertips and easily accessible. Every aspect of human life has been touched and affected by modern culture from our relationships to the earth, to our relationships with each other, our cosmos, God and any and everything in between. Somewhere along the way in this amazing journey, we've lost touch with something. There is a lost connection to ourselves, to our communities, and to a greater understanding of what it is to be a human living with other humans on planet earth.

In a relatively short period of time, we have developed a very different way of life than our recent ancestors had. It's staggering, really, to consider that as recently as 50 years ago we were living very different lives than most of us in the western world are living now. I am most certainly grateful for the opportunities that I have had in my life that the technology and advances of the past century have brought, and certainly am not going to be one who says, "Let's go back in time." The "good old days" may seem ideal and attractive to those scourged by modern culture, but the fantasy is always better than the reality. Most people in today's world would find it very challenging to live the way our great grandparents did. I do, however, advocate taking the best of all worlds possible and being more active and creative with how we move into the future. Especially since we now have the wisdom of the past and the whole world at our fingertips, along with the technology to project into the future to understand the potential impacts of practically any chosen course of action! It would seem purely ignorant to not begin to cultivate a middle ground that integrates what works into our world, and carefully removes those pieces that are causing sickness, disease and malignancies.

"Our value system is backwards. It focuses on money, materialism and self centeredness. It affects me all day, every day. Sometimes with little intensity other times with great intensity. It hurts to have to feel like I must do something with my time that does not serve myself and/ or my community in order to fulfill this backwards value system."
Aimee Miller

Fortunate or not, in any rapid development, some things are more carefully thought out than others. In the wild enthusiasm of "Progress," and it's good friend "Capitalism," much seems to have been overlooked or ignored in relationship to the human system and our environment. "Progress" it would seem, took on a life of it's own and in machine like fashion has created a bit of a monster out of itself, in strong partnership with capitalism and consumerism. The effects of this are widespread and truly too vast to go into in any significant depth here. It's a story that's being told everywhere now. They include physical effects on our ecosystems, effects to the human system (biological, sociological, neurological, etc.), and global effects to our precious planet.

In Ecology, "Indicator" species help scientists to understand what is happening in an ecosystem by how those indicator species are being affected and adapting, or not adapting. If each of us were to look around in our lives at the individuals we know and see regularly, we could get a fair idea of what some of the most prevalent symptoms are that modern culture has been manifesting. The individual is the "indicator" species, if you will, of a culture, and while there will always be deviations to any norm, we can start to get an idea of the overall health of our community, culture and planet by observing what's going on in ourselves and in those we know.

Depression, Overwhelm and Individual Symptoms

It seems when I share with my friends and family, these common themes keep repeating: I feel disconnected, isolated, depressed, grieved by the state of the world, I long for community, I feel alone, lost in a techno sea of insanity, I'm tired. There is this underlying feeling of being "overwhelmed" in life. Life is "crazy" or "too much," or "I can't keep up," just seem to be normal every day phrases I hear everywhere I go and from practically everyone who is participating in modern culture. In the grocery store, on the phone with people I know, walking by someone on the streets, or in the café: I hear it everywhere, and I see the symptoms of it in myself as well as all around me.

Jenny Sustello, from Boulder sent this sharing to me while I was in Hawaii writing this book. Jenny is a good friend of mine, and is the single mom of a beautiful young woman named Taylor. Jenny really lays it out, and I think her voice speaks for many of us in today's world.

"Overstimulated/overvigilant/overwhelmed/overworked/ overseperated/overconfused/overbusy/overconcerned/overwounded/ overtaxed/overterrorized/overdebted over the top of too much. I wonder if we have come to a time of too much of a good thing or a not so good thing."

"To me it comes across as what could be felt as Post Traumatic Stress Disorder. Sometimes I look around when I am out in society and feel like I am in the twilight zone or something. Then I wonder if I am just going nuts or if all this is really happening? Perhaps it is a bit of both. I think at times, "Ok we can turn this train around, together," and in others I feel like "Whoa we are so off course and things are so off balance now it would take a gazzilion years to reverse this thing." Then I remember how long people just like us have marched onward, soldiers for peace and justice, and yet we are still here now and worse. Indeed some things have gotten done, and some great changes have taken place throughout history by some amazing souls. Still I am concerned that each day the world spins around in this "business as usual" way and the huge cries and crisis are not being heard or addressed. Money, production, growth, performance and stock markets are sometimes not the most important issues here to focus all our energy and attention on. Especially when the very thing we are working so very hard for or towards, (or at least a lot of us hope to accomplish in our lives) is the very thing that is escaping us by all the ridiculous pressures, demands, sickness and expectations in this society. We seem to have lost connection with the sacred of life and the empowerment of healthy intentional living: the very substance we are here to experience.

"It appears we have a pill out there to pop for anything and everything these days. Insanity. Is this what we and our families have been reduced to: drugged out, checked out, addicted and numbed out? Are these the lives we were meant to live? I look around me and see people lost, as if we can't remember our way because we have forgotten where we came from, don't realize the realness and importance of where we are at, and have lost sight of our direction to where we are going.

"Sometimes I wonder if the broken record of our history and current issues have been the experience and 'theme' on this planet thus far. For what seems like for the majority of us, this life has left lots of battle wounds. What is really going on here? Seems strange to me really, when I take a deeper look at it. Is this all we know? Can we as the masses ever rise above these energies, limitations and suppressions that keep us down? Is it possible to break these vicious cycles in our world, in our minds? I sure hope so. Maybe this is where the level of impact of intensity is valuable: feeling deep in our heart and souls the pain and grief that comes from all of this will be enough to catapult us onward and upward... somehow someway someday...

"And in the midst of it all, it is as if some race against time is occurring. Now more than ever we should be allowed to have a more gentler and reflective lifestyle. I wonder what my child and others children will be left with or having to go through because of the extreme raping and pilfering of our mother earth that has taken place over the recent years. Then there are all these very sad business deals that are based only on making money. They do not think twice about what they are selling to us or our kids. How they are toxifying our earth, bodies and minds with their ways and products that are being marketed and advertised to their fellow human family. It's pathetic really. The repercussions do not end at the dollar money making deal.

"Very sadly enough I think the effects of all these things provide perfect breeding ground for a neurotic sort of human race. It appears that this world highly values each of us keeping quite busy and making sure we are always 'doing' something. What ever happened to just "being?" People are now being requested to work their jobs 40 - 60 hours per week. What time or energy is left for them to care for themselves, their homes, families, and communities? Sometimes I look around and it seems insane. This frenetic pace and schedule we keep our selves and families under. I know for myself I need enough recovery time after working a chaotic and hectic work week just to be OK, not even good yet. I think that could be said across the board. Trying to keep our spirits up and our souls alive each day. Wondering what we can possibly do at this point to help the direction of our world positively while we are feeling as if we are swimming up steam. Feeling as if lost at sea and disconnected too much of the time, being tossed to and fro in this stormy sea and seeking a refuge, a rescue team, a light house anywhere in sight...

"Overconsumerized/overchemicalized/overrushed/overtechnolized/overcontrolled/overbrainwashed/overscheduled/overpopulated/overdrugged.

"Praying intently for divine direction and help within these times of uncertainty. What to believe in, who to believe in, what to invest our time, money and energy in. Perhaps this is all part of this grand dream, which feels like bouts of nightmares in between. Wondering if we are powerful or powerless, and what do we have control over and what do we not? Are we God and Goddess or are we victims, experiment projects, slaves, robots?

"I have experienced both or something in between, however. I do feel spun up in this web like matrix that appears to be a creation of sorts by something or someone who exists within the energies of war, destruction, control, egoism, coldness, hardness, raping, pilfering, power struggles, greed, enslavement, suppression, depression, oppression, hierarchy, patriarchy, highly polluted earth, water and air, and attempted brainwashing. And this is all just the tip of the iceberg of what's happening within and around us.

"What my heart and soul cry out for is the total opposite. To live in an environment and experience of softness, support, unconditional love, warmth, grace, contentment, enough, safety, gentleness, beauty, innocence, true freedom, balance, sacredness, nurturing, peace, empowerment, celebration, and equality.

"I feel almost trapped here in this place. It feels like a no win situation no matter how hard I try, no matter how many hours per week I work, no matter how much money I save or how much I could place into the stock market. I feel I am working for something that feels like smoke and mirrors. Maybe I am really missing something huge here. Hopefully one day it is all going to just make clear sense and everything will come together beautifully.

"I am very curious what the cure is. I just want to be who and what I am - always, and for those around me to feel safe and supported to be the same. To be more than ok in this world. I pray for a time when each of us are living in our full true nature and essence, present powerful and alive with all of life. I wonder if a world like this is possible or exists?"

Jenny Sustello, Boulder, CO

When I was growing up, my mother always said, "I'm just so tired." As an adult, I can now understand why and I see the effect that the ever quickening pace of life has had on her over the years. She worked full time, raised two children, managed 30 odd units of rentals, cooked all our meals and somehow managed to be up every morning by 5:30 to do it all over again. She had no community, no one to ask to help for anything, and though my father was living with us, it was rarely an option for her to even ask him to help, as he was also working so much and not really available to support her in those ways. The messages that I got, as a child, were very clear, "You need something done, do it yourself. Art and play are a waste of time. You can't count on anyone but yourself. You have to be strong, life is work, and work isn't fun, and it's out of the question to ask for help for anything. Don't show your emotion, never cry, money always comes first, and money is the objective of life, get as much as you can, hold onto it and don't let anyone know what you've got. Everyone else is out to get you and you can't trust anyone." I mean really, that was what got shown to me at a very young age, certainly not consciously, but at a deep sub-conscious level, those were the messages I got, and it came from everywhere: family, TV, school, and the whole culture I was in.

My family was the classic American story: the single family trying to make it in the world and provide something for their children that was better than what they had. My father worked all day with an hour commute each way, and didn't even want to talk to us by the time he got home, he was so overwhelmed with taxes, the rentals, and whatever unknown stresses he had at his job as an aeronautical engineer. He always seemed angry, upset, or like maybe he'd just pop, so everyone was kind of afraid of him, which I'm sure only made him feel more isolated and alone in his pain. As a child, of course, this is terrifying to experience. As an adult, I've learned deep compassion and understanding for what my parents must have been feeling, because I can easily see how this world pushes us into a very unhealthy relationship with time, resources and our families. This was 30 years ago. Now the intensity of keeping up is even more demanding on every level, and the reality is few people have any kind of support network, or community. Even for those who do, it's hard to ask friends, because their friends are also overwhelmed, super busy and just scraping by to maintain and no one wants to stress out their friends more. Many people don't even have many friends out side of work, there just isn't enough time to create social bonds or nurture them. Relationships take time and energy. Many people can barely maintain one with their significant other, much less numerous deep and meaningful relationships in community because there just isn't enough time for them to truly grow and develop in their busy lives.

While I was in Kauai preparing for my writing time for this project, a friend of mine, Archer, broke it down really clearly. The average working person has a 14 hour day to just maintain their lives and maybe exercise a little or shop for necessities/food, etc. That's before even thinking about anything extra like socializing or music. He's looking at the 8-5 model here and assuming an hour (min) commute each way, many people commute much longer. An hour to get ready, eat, shower, etc for work, two hours a day commuting, eight hours work, two more hours for meals (lunch, and dinner), and an hour for exercise. That's 14 hours before thinking about spending time with our families, exploring our passions or artistic callings, taking care of bills, and household responsibilities, parenting or anything at all extra. Considering 8 hours sleep is a good healthy dose, that leaves the average working person with maybe 2 hours to indulge in personal time, build relationships and nurture our connections to self, others and source. Of course people are feeling crunched, popping pills to numb the pain, and going crazy.

Life is moving fast. Technology has us frying our brains with cell phones, computers, TV screens and a virtual constant bombardment from wireless frequencies in every café, home and public building. The demands on our wallets are increasing faster by far than the wage. The media is filling us with images of death, destruction and global devastation and rarely reports anything positive that inspires us. Our world is at war, the future for our children is intense and scary, global warming is imminent and many of us seriously wonder if our government is indeed a democracy "By the people for the people." The people are, for the most part, so overwhelmed by trying to survive that few notice or have the energy left to care, much less be pro-active in trying to change things. Plenty of people feel and live in the reality of "Me against the world" in their minds and feel the effects of isolation and "individualism" to it's extreme.

Depression, anxiety, and what I personally have begun to call "Overwhelm Syndrome" are increasingly common in all ages of people today and create an increased feeling of "aloneness" in those who suffer from it. The World Health Organization says that depression is among the leading causes of disability worldwide. An estimated 5.8% of men and 9.5% of women world-wide will experience a depressive episode in any given year, and an estimated 121 million people world-wide currently suffer from depression. Approximately 18.8 million American adults have depression and more than 19 million American adults have an anxiety disorder according to the National Institute of Mental Health.

One of the most commonly shared experiences in those suffering from depression, anxiety and overwhelm is the feeling of being "lonely," or isolated, or the feeling of not fitting in with the way the "world is." Breathing Space of Scotland (www.breathingspacescotland. co.uk) says, "This comes with living in a world where certain "ways of being" have come to be expected. You might feel isolated if you cannot celebrate or show part of your identity." In addition, a lack of opportunities to "get involved or "participate" contributes greatly to a sense of worthlessness, aloneness and isolation. (Breathing Space)

"All the lonely people, where do they all come from?"
I share this feeling of being perplexed at the sheer volume of people who are dealing with feelings of intense loneliness and depression in America. I personally know dozens of people, with seemingly normal and fulfilling lives, who are taking medication for depression.

"Twenty years ago, I rarely heard of depression. Now it is an American pandemic. I believe this phenomenon is a product of our society and overall mind set. We are conditioned from childhood to be fiercely individualistic and self-centered in order to survive. We are taught that the basis of a meaningful life is personal achievement. In many other societies the welfare of the whole community is the focal point, and cooperation is the means to the end. In American society, the success of the individual is most important, and competition is the means to the end. Deep and meaningful relationships (love) with other people are second at best on the list of our priorities. They are often never wholeheartedly sought and or given the extraordinary amount of time and effort we expend towards personal achievement. If they are developed, many often fade from neglect.

"Loneliness and feelings of isolation are widespread in our society for a reason: We ARE lonely and isolated, if not physically then emotionally. Our hearts won't lie to us, they hurt for a reason. They are being deprived of the most meaningful thing in this life at the expense of the most meaningless."
Neville Palmer

As Neville makes clear, we don't need a psychologist or sociologist to tell us that the modern world's way of life has taken a toll on the human experience. We can all find examples of it's effects in our lives if we look around even a little, or maybe, if you're like me, you may only have to look in the mirror some days to see it. We have lost, for the most part, a sense of community and of "belonging" to something greater than ourselves in the rush for survival and independence.

"Communities no longer see themselves as groups of people concerned with others, and no longer have the discipline needed to attain a common vision. Many present-day communities consist of groups of isolated individuals struggling to relate to the demands of urbanization and industrialization, having withdrawn and become isolated from meaningfully taking part in world society. The effect of loss of a sense of destiny, isolationism and a failure to live beyond the moment is also illustrated in the collapse of the family as a unit." (UIA)

There are so many repercussions to the above statement, and though there is plenty of research out there to support this, we need only look directly at our own lives to see it clearly. Going straight to home as a starting point, and expanding out, we can easily start to see the levels of disconnection that are so silently woven into the fabric of modern life. How is it that we live? Do we know our neighbors? And in that, I don't mean do we know their first names, and wave to them when we go down the street happening to cross paths on our way to work, but do we *know* them? Do we know how they interact with others, what their stresses are, how they discipline their children or what kinds of spices they like in their foods?

What is the purpose of our lives? Are we working just to pay bills and keep the car running? Do we daily get to feel that the contributions we make actually count for something greater than ourselves? Is life fulfilling or just a routine we accept as the "misery of life" because that's what mainstream modern culture shows us as the be all end all, chasing the dream of "someday." "Someday" being this illusionary supposed "goal" of the American Dream with a nice house, two cars, two kids and a retirement fund. What many people find when they get there is a deepened experience of loneliness, isolation and lack of community.

The overall breakdown of community in the modern world is a huge topic in today's world and many people are commenting on it's effects worldwide. It is a real epidemic and spreading like wild to all parts of the world. With the continuing disappearance of the traditional lifestyles of native populations, the dis-ease of modern culture is making it's mark everywhere. The Union of International Associations (UIA) – non-profit, apolitical, independent, and non-governmental – is an extraordinary scientific research institute and documentation centre. It focuses on a topic of increasing relevance: the nature and evolution of international civil society. In their discussions on the breakdown of community, they examine many facets of what is happening as a result of the modernization of our world. "People seek the purpose of existence in their work, family, society, and cultural tradition, many of which no longer give meaning. As a part of real, everyday experience, people in the 20th Century have seen many of the understandings that gave meaning to their hopes and ambitions collapse. While in the midst of bitter disillusionments and painful failures in aspiration, the individual comes to doubt his own creative worth in society. Nevertheless, a deep desire for creative action is retained. The more doubts there are, the stronger the desire to express creatively while the experience of futility impels the destruction of others' creations. There is a collapse in the meaningfulness of social participation and a lack of opportunities for the same. "

When we add in the effects of more and more people working from home on their computers, not even having the basic socialization and camaraderie that a workplace environment can provide, the reality that you can shop from home, not even needing to leave the house for getting basic necessities, and the lack of healthy community hubs or centers that are offering interesting and exciting events or gatherings, it becomes easy to see how people can begin to feel alone, lost and alienated from each other. There are volumes being written on this social and global "crisis" and the Lost Connection is a study in and of itself. It gets really deep when we look at the possibilities of how and why it is being allowed to continue, even when the research and our personal lives reflect the obvious severity of the symptoms pointing towards a systemic infection, even when it is clear that we are nearing a breaking point of the human spirit, or, we may wonder, is that indeed the point? Do we need to break in order to see the deeper reality of the human experience and return to a way of life that is sustainable and interactive?

Effects on our Children

"As they grow, children become the manifestation of the many institutions which educate and influence them. Culture expresses all that a society is, and children, as they absorb this culture, will become that in it's entirety." (Orford)

Sociologists are noting the effects of this way of life on all ages of people, but are seeing some of the most intense effects, of course, on our children. It is estimated that between 10-25% of children suffer from one or more mental illnesses today. Children are our indicator population for the future, and the health of our children will definitely impact the health of our world in the coming years, as they become the adult population. "One in five children has a diagnosable mental, emotional or behavioral disorder. And up to one in 10 may suffer from a serious emotional disturbance. Attention deficit hyperactivity disorder (ADD) is one of the most commonly diagnosed mental disorders in children, affecting 3 to 5 percent of school-age children (NIMH, 1999). As many as one in every 33 children and one in eight adolescents may have depression (CMHS, 1998). At any point in time, 10 to 15 percent of children have some symptoms of depression. (SAMHSA, CMHS, 2003: Major Depression in Children and Adolescents Fact Sheet) Major depression strikes about 1 in 12 adolescents. Among those adolescents that develop major depression, 1 in 14 will commit suicide as a young adult. (Source: Weissman, et.al., Depressed Adolescents All Grown Up, JAMA. 1999 281, 1701-13.) Suicide is the third leading cause of death for 15- to 24-year-olds and the sixth leading cause of death for 5- to 14-year-olds. The number of attempted suicides is even higher (AACAP, 1997)." (Sokolova) In 2004, more than 5,000 U.S. children and adolescents committed suicide and an additional 171,870 non-fatal self-harm injury cases were reported. (CDC, National Center for Injury Prevention and Control)

According to a study published in the journal Psychiatric Services, April 2004, at least four percent of pre-schoolers, over a million, are clinically depressed and many are put on anti-depressants at a very young age.(Lachance) This in and of itself deserves a serious look as a symptom of something wrong! The part that scares me the most in this is that there are no real long term studies on the impacts and "side" effects of these drugs over the course of a lifetime. I have met a few adults who were put on Ritalin as youngsters, and they have shared that it has been a very difficult life experience to deal with, and that they feel deeply that those drugs messed them up permanently, mentally, spiritually and emotionally, and now they are on a hard core healing path to try to detoxify their bodies and find natural ways to deal with the long lasting effects that these childhood prescription drugs have had on them.

Drugging our children has become commonplace and accepted in mainstream culture as an easier and quicker fix than really looking deeper at the underlying causes contributing to these issues. Ritalin, Prozac and many other prescribed drugs are now regular part of our children's lives, and yet we have big campaigns that say, "Just say no to drugs." It's got to be a bit confusing for them, drugs are drugs right? I could see a young adult easily justifying drugs in today's world. If mom's giving them to me, they must be OK from my friends too, right? So the campaign and the slogans are meaningless really in today's world for our children; it's hypocrisy really. These drugs cause serious long and short-term side effects including liver damage, and still aren't dealing with the root causes of their issues. Dr. Barry Bittman at the Health Rhythms conference I attended in 2003 stated, "Side effects are known definite effects of a drug, it's a very misleading term. Side effects are the proven physiological responses that are guaranteed to occur in subjects over time." How can we be advocating and allowing this and not expect our future world to bear the repercussions as our children become adults? What kind of adults are they going to be if they are taught that a pill is the answer to their problems before they're even in grade school? What are the long-term implications to a child's overall well being throughout their lives, and should we not be seriously considering this in the future of our world?

In an article published in the Telegraph News in the UK, a group of concerned child development specialists and teachers got together to try to address this issue and ask for government support in creating a healthier world and future for our children. "A sinister cocktail of junk food, prescription drugs, marketing, over-competitive schooling and electronic entertainment is poisoning childhood. Since children's brains are still developing, they cannot adjust to the effects of ever more rapid technological and cultural change. They still need what developing human beings have always needed, including real food (as opposed to processed "junk"), real play (as opposed to sedentary, screen-based entertainment), first-hand experience of the world they live in and regular interaction with the real-life significant adults in their lives. They also need time. In a fast-moving, hyper-competitive culture, today's children are expected to cope with an ever-earlier start to formal schoolwork and an overly academic test-driven primary curriculum. They are pushed by market forces to act and dress like mini-adults and exposed via the electronic media to material that would have been considered unsuitable for children even in the very recent past. Children have been put into an academic straitjacket from a very early age which restricts creativity and the enrichment of childhood."(Fenton)
Our children are our future, and if they are also sickened and isolated,

then our infection is real and much more long lasting, possibly permanent. This issue is deep into the place of needing desperate attention, treatment and effective strategies to bring the entire human system back into a healthy balance. In my life, I have seen very few individuals or communities that have not been affected by the symptoms of modern techno cultural and the global epidemic it is spawning in one way or another. That includes myself, as well as my friends, and my family in every way.

How did we get so lost?

Different Breed

Sometimes I think I'm a different breed
I don't even like what they say I oughta need
I don't like TV, and I don't drink coke
When I look at the world, I pray it's a joke
Maybe evolution just passed me by
Me, I'm just sitting here wondering why

Sometimes I think I'm from a different place
Maybe far away, in outer space
Maybe just from a time gone past
For me this world moves much too fast
I can't even keep up with yesterday
I got tomorrow knocking at my front door
Saying "Gimme gimme gimme gimme more
More money, more time,
Give me a little piece of your mind.

"What has this place come to?
Where have my people gone?
I see them in the forest
Away from the concrete and neon
Maybe I'm from a different place
Maybe I'm a different breed."
                    Cheri Shanti, Visions of Reality CD c2000

At least once a day I am either involved in or hear a conversation on the state of our world, and always the question arises, "How did it get to this point?" How did we get so separated, so isolated from not only each other, but from the very essence of our selves as humans? How did we lose touch and forget how to connect? I know that I cannot even begin to touch the scope and breadth of that question in this book, much less in one chapter. Just as the symptoms previously mentioned are just a small representation of the vastness of a huge condition, there is much to be said in relation to how it got so crazy. I am truly only just scratching the surface on all levels of these concerns.

These issues go deep into our history, and into the human psyche. Fear is a significant consideration, and I feel that a lot of what has arisen, somehow, if we traced it back, would be rooted in a fear of something. A fear of lack of food, a fear of lack of money or resources, a fear of those who are different and believed in different Gods, a fear of being dominated, a fear of working too hard, a fear of not enough work, fears of being alone, fears of being together, fears of the Gods, fears of our environment, fear of catastrophe, fear of death. There are innumerable relationships we can draw on which form a colossal web of potential creative forces that have led us to our present situation.

I believe, like any epidemic or crisis condition, that there are inestimable interwoven factors that contribute and that it is a whole book or more in and of itself to really examine this question fully. History, politics, cultural heritage, technology, media, spirituality, religion and the history of the religion, socio-economic stressors and factors, values of a people, and of individuals who hold influence (like politicians or social activists), regional variables like environment and what it demands or provides, infrastructures and more have played a part in sculpting our present reality and will undoubtedly play a role in our future. Sociologists go into much more depth on these issues than I will in this book, and there are countless explanations, theories and studies which, in my humble opinion, all have some validity and add up to the sum of "now here!"

Greed and need have always been challenges for every population and culture to deal with on some level, and it must be recognized that different "factions" or socio-economic groups, of a population have different intentions/needs/desires than others. Kings, presidents and people making decisions for a nation have much different agendas and concerns than a dairy farmer, or a mom in middle America, or tribal kinsmen who just want to survive the next season and feed their families in peace. Fortunate or not, often and usually, those who are making the decisions for the common people are often not considering long term repercussions to the common people, nor are they really in touch with what they want and need to prosper or how their decisions affect their people on the streets. Often, they simply don't care to know. I recently read a humorous story in one of Boulder's local papers that is a great example of this. During a press conference with president Bush, a reporter had asked him to talk a little about gas prices. The reporter was expressing the concern of Americans that prices were nearing $4.00 a gallon in many places around the country. Bush's response was that he had no idea gas prices were getting close to $4.00 a gallon, he hadn't been made aware of that and he was shocked. He is in complete ignorance to what is happening in the lives of everyday people in his own country! Of course it won't affect him, he probably never goes to the pumps and certainly doesn't pay for his gas the same way most American's do.

Everything that is happening now is a result of choices made that, at the time, probably seemed to be the best and most beneficial choices for those making the decisions. I don't subscribe to the thought that there is some evil force at work trying to destroy the human connection, though I do think that the manifestation that has occurred is becoming sort of it's own "beast" or machine, with it's own unconscious agenda. I like to think that most leaders and people inherently do the best that they can at the time with the knowledge and wisdom that is available to them. I also feel strongly that most of them see reality thru a much different lens than the common person on the streets or in the village. While they may think or even whole-heartedly believe that they're doing the best for their people, they may be doing the worst. Where they think they will alleviate pain and suffering, they cause twice as much, where they think they will bring peace, they bring war and revenge that lasts generations upon generations. What they consider to be in our best interest may very well be twisted and convoluted in their minds as to how it best serves their political or financial agendas.

The industrial revolution, at the time, seemed like the best thing ever. It offered a way to make life easier and create more free time, more abundance, more "stuff" etc. We all know that hindsight is 20/20. At that time there simply wasn't the information, forethought, or systems in place that could show the people what is now so clearly evident. I wonder, if they knew that it would pollute and damage our eco-systems to the point of no return, require huge financial resources to clean up it's messes, create a way of life that is now requiring more time and energy than it offers, eat up the resources of our planet, create cancers in our bodies and make a machine out of us, would they have done things differently? I would like to think that yes, there would have been more conscious deliberation on creating a sustainable future where our children would have clean water, air and real food to eat that isn't polluted with chemicals and the possibility of a peaceful co-existence with nature rather than a mad rush to try to save what little is left.

And now, with the Technological Revolution, we have another set of factors to consider in how the individual is affected thru modern culture. There are so many gadgets to keep up with, i-phones, laptops, wireless everything, a million options for each and a whole world of education around staying on top of the trends so that you can keep at least a virtual connection, since there may not be enough time to have real face to face connection anymore. All of this takes time and energy away from real and personal social interaction, feeding ourselves, exploring nature, staring at the stars and pondering the mysteries of life, etc. How many people have even stopped to consider the potential affects or consequences on the human system neurologically and biologically from these electromagnetically charged devices? The silent and unstated reality is that there is very little research on the long term affects of these "conveniences" to the human bio-system, and the research is growing to prove that indeed we are affected by EMFs and there is some limit to what our bodies should be exposed to on any kind of consistent basis.

In January, 2005 the National Radiological Protection Board announced that they are advising parents to not allow cell phone use by children under the age of 8 as research conducted in the past 5 years strongly suggests there are harmful effects to the developing brain from the EMFs coming from a cell phone, and that they can disrupt learning patterns, memory retention and more. Other studies done in Europe and the US support this and talk about the increased incidence in brain tumors, and a whole host of other health hazards that cell phones are now being linked to, including learning disabilities for children. Cell phones are glued to everyone's ears at all ages, and people are developing strange tumors on the sides of their faces near where the phone sits, getting headaches, feeling the "heat" of the phone when they use it too long and having feelings of anxiety increase in high

Electromagnetic zones, like cities or malls. Yet, still cell phones are replacing land lines everywhere, and we are indeed paying with our hard earned dollars, for our own demise and disease and even still considering it an irreplaceable convenience. Very few people take it very seriously.

It's like we're being trained to be quiet obedient sheep. Partially it's out of overwhelm and not wanting to have to be inconvenienced; we go for whatever modern culture gives us that lets us move faster and be "on the go" more effectively. We go for it, hook line and sinker, following the trend laid out before us once again, not using any forethought of what this may be planting the seeds for in our world and in the world of our children. Not questioning "authority" or the "majority" too much really, just assuming, "Well, if the government approves Cell phones, they must be OK for little Johnny in grade school and it makes it so much easier for me." It's offered as such a great service and indeed has made our ability to work remotely and travel while staying in touch much easier, but we're going just as blindly into the possibility of more disease and damage as did those who were so enthusiastic about the industrial revolution. Like any systemic infection, it starts slowly and if not treated or addressed spreads throughout the entirety of the system over time, often undetectable for years until symptoms are suddenly erupting everywhere.

The Information Age that we're deeply imbedded in now, had it been always present, might have held the power to help people make better decisions throughout modern history. As a good friend of mine likes to say, "It is what it is," and so we now must simply move forward and deal with the repercussions of the decisions that our parents, and their parents, made in their ignorance of the need to preserve our planet and the greater global good we are now seeking to serve. I'm not using the word ignorance here in any kind of negative connotation, or with any blame. The reality was, at that time the information wasn't available to know what we know now, and the world seemed so big, so abundant, so able to take whatever we could do to it, those generations simply didn't think about the inevitable possibilities we are looking at now of polluted water, dead seas, overly processed and treated foods, etc. Hopefully, we can begin to learn from their mistakes and make better choices so our children can find harmony and peaceful co-existence in their lives.

The Collapse of Community

There are a variety of definitions for community. It can be defined as a group of people who happen to live close to each other like housing communities, or as a group of people with common interests or backgrounds; loosely it can be just the public or society in general. I am looking at community from a combined perspective of all of that. Life has taught me that there is a need to realize, in today's world, that we do indeed form a global community of humans who are now sharing resources, skills and energy worldwide. In order to serve this larger community effectively and consciously, we have to look first at how we interact as individuals in our daily lives, in our daily smaller communities: at work, at home and in our town. Community is the backbone of a culture. In community we learn how to relate to each other, how to be together, how to effectively work together, resolve conflict and create solutions. We can witness others and learn valuable life lessons thru the experiences of others. Without community, we are isolated and often lose touch with how to share and work together as humans. Community also fosters a sense of mutual respect, and is a very effective means of modifying and controlling deviant behavior.

I've been blessed to be able to travel quite a bit since I was 15 years old to other countries and experience first hand the way other cultures work, live and express. I've spent a few years total time in third world countries around the world and while that may not be much, it is enough to have some interesting realizations and learn a lot. During college, I did a study abroad internship in the Turks and Caicos Islands in the Caribbean Sea on an island called South Caicos. I lived there for a total of about 6 months as an intern for a Marine Ecology course. The island is pretty small, it takes less than two hours to bike across it. The thing I remember the most is how safe I felt there. Much safer than I ever did in Florida where I grew up and went to school, much safer than anywhere I'd ever felt in my own country. I found this to be true in many of the third world countries I've visited, including India. On S. Caicos, I had befriended one of the islanders; his name was "Ganger." He was much like a big brother to me, always helping me out, and he worked with me on the boats with the students at times too. He and I would talk late into the night, and often we'd talk about the massive social problems of the world and how to effect change. One night we were talking about crime and domestic violence. I asked him what the crime rate was like there, and he said, "Not a problem ya know. Nobody wants to get kicked off dee island. Here, you do something wrong, dey put you in a boat, sail you out to sea, you can never come back. You show up at another island, mon, they want to know what you done wrong at home to have to leave."

In 2006 I went to Guatemala to drum and hold ceremony with a group there during a Solstice Ritual at the pyramids of Tikal. While we were there, in the village we were staying in, a villager had been caught stealing for the third time from someone else in the community. He had been warned and excused twice already for stealing in the recent past. The people dealt with things in their own way there. Calling the police just isn't the tribal way; it's not even a consideration. In tight tribal communities, the people rule themselves. This man was taken to a field and, with the entire community of villagers present, including his wife and family, he was punished publicly. The message to the tribe was clearly felt by all present.

Now, while I certainly don't advocate either of these particular methods, or any methodology that promotes fear, my point is that when people know they have to live together and be held accountable by their entire community for their actions, they are less likely to cross the lines of respect and good behavior. Crime just simply isn't a concept in many tribal communities because of the strength of the connection the people need to have to survive and thrive. When people are expected to act with a certain dignity and respect and know that they will be held accountable when they don't, they just rise to the occasion more naturally. They want to be respected and they want to be included, and for many in the second and third worlds, their very survival, and the survival of their families depends on it, so again, there is another powerful social regulator. Of course, there are and always will be deviations from the norm, but in smaller communities it is harder to "get away with murder" or any other criminal behavior for that matter. There is much more transparency and personal accountability than what we have created here in the west.

In the Western world, where people live isolated lives in little apartments tucked away from each other, it becomes easy for a deviant mind to think there are no consequences, that it won't matter, they can hide out, be invisible, and think that it doesn't matter what they do, no one will notice. Stealing from stores doesn't seem like it would affect anyone, the corporation has lots of money, pilfering money from people on line is easier since you never have to see the person: it's impersonal easy theft! Child abuse and sexual misconduct behind closed doors in our safe little boxes is easy to hide and lie about since there is often no "proof" or no "witnesses." Criminal minds and activities can thrive in a culture that doesn't provide for personal accountability or consequence, where the system has gotten so big, it's easy to slip thru the cracks unnoticed, and where justice takes years to complete. In communities, people hold each other accountable and take on the task of immediate justice thru council and gathering the entire community to witness the wrong doer, and decide how to either re-integrate them, teach them better, or move them out.

The Union of International Associates talks about the deterioration of communities and the overall non-participation of individuals within communities as one of the most pressing and significant Global problems of our time and is listed on their website under World Problems. "The collapse in the meaningfulness of social participation and a lack of opportunities for participation began around the turn of the century. By the end of World War I this collapse was nearly complete. World War II, in fact, revived a sense of meaning for the western world. The values of decency, humanity, civilization, material and technological progress came to be seen as forces of good. For the individual, normalcy and uniformity were considered good and religious yearnings; neuroses or deviation from convention were regarded as a pathological condition. Society was not so much for something as against "Communism," and a poorly defined communism at that."

"By the mid-1960s these values were discredited for the most part. The youth were flaunting abnormality as a source of pride; the abnormal became the creative or the self-expressive. The social upheavals of the civil rights movement, the anti-Vietnam war movement, and the student uprising of Paris and else where exposed the hollowness of materialistic consumerism. Once again there was no positive direction, except survival and muddling through, which had become goals in themselves. Many people felt hopeless, desperate and lost in this time, feeling that there was nothing good in the future to believe in. Without a belief in the future, the present becomes the focus of the search for purpose. Yet, even the present is being questioned now." (UIA)

And rightfully so; we have to question a way of life that has so quickly and dramatically increased the incidence of mental illness, depression, anxiety, and the overall breakdown of the family as well as community structure. More significantly, finding creative ways of bringing people together again is imperative to the next stage of our evolution as humans on the planet. In this next evolution, we get to make the choices that will impact future generations. Since we do now have the ease of access to pertinent information, along with forethought and the great wisdom of hindsight, we inevitably have the ability to make much better decisions now than at any other time in history. We are now armed with the wisdom of the whole world's lessons at our fingertips, thru the power of the Internet, as well as the power of technology to look at futuristic prediction models. There will be no excuse for us of ignorance due to lack of information as there has been for past generations!

There are countless possibilities, and again, many facets to consider in this evolution. Re-educating each other and our greater communities, families and tribes, bringing awareness to what will happen if we don't find creative solutions, (which the media and internet are doing on many levels) and exploring/creating alternatives to what is being offered by "mainstream" culture are crucial aspects on every level from social issues to economic issues, from how we spend our time being "entertained" to how we participate in creating the world we live in and that our children will inherit. Each of the factors listed at the beginning of this section that have contributed to our current state must be addressed individually and in relationship to each other. Decisions need to now be made considering future generations and not just the easiest, most profitable, quickest fix. We've learned already where that road will take us, the time now is to explore how to use the best of all of it and integrate the modern with the ancient, community with strong independent individuals, and creativity with discipline.

The good news is that depression, anxiety, community deterioration, lack of social participation and all of the conditions and symptoms of modern culture, can be transformed on all levels with attention and intention. Music and music making are one of many possibilities towards helping us find more balance in our lives. In my experience, it is the human connection that heals beyond any pill, drug, or procedure. It is the human connection that we have lost and it is the human connection that must be re-wired to move us forward. Music is one way that we can begin to weave the threads of our humanness together!

Chapter 2

Music:

A Human Connection

"I love how music is such a good way to connect to the human race."
Lauren Clark, Boulder, CO

"Music and dance are the multidimensional languages of the soul. Only they can successfully communicate the FEELING of human. Only they can communicate the emotions of what it means to be more than human. Only they can send a reciprocal feedback of vibrations that may manifest our deepest feelings with otherworldly sentience and lay out a field of possibilities for what's to come. This multi-dimensional reciprocality is the language of the future, which we are creating together right now. Thought manifests silently, language communicates linearly, but music and the movement of dance speak on a multi-dimensional level that encompasses us whole. Let us evolve together, for there is so much to create, so much to feel, so much to become."

Stephiniti

"Music is a language that everyone speaks. Rhythm has the potential to harmonize, unify and take us to a new world that could promote peace, harmony and human connection."
Christine Stevens

The human connection: an indescribable experience that is necessary for the health and well being of any individual. It has been defined as the interaction between humans, also the interaction between humans and our environments, between humans and the divine, as recognition of each other as thinking and feeling beings, and as the vital social education that we need in order to survive and thrive in community. It defies full definition, as some part of it is more of a feeling, a deep inner awareness that one is not alone, that there are others sharing in the multi-dimensional experience of being human. It's what makes us cry in a touching scene in a movie, or feel angry about injustice to someone we may not even know personally in a land far away, or even a time gone past. It is what makes us concerned for the future of our planet and our children.

The human connection is that place in us that resonates with the experiences of others, and that can "feel" the pain or the joy of someone else's reality. The human connection can never be replaced by technology and can have no real or effective substitute in our lives. The virtual world, connecting "online," is trying to provide a piece of it, but virtual connection simply can not take the place of real face to face sharing and being together. It is this basic human need that our modern world is robbing us of on many levels, and it is the deep and undying inner desire for it that is pushing us to seek out more and new ways to connect. For some it is going to bars, for others it is church, for still others it may be the country clubs or social groups of some kind, regardless of the direction we go to seek it out, it is, always has been and will be, a natural part of our being as a social species.

Music has always had tremendous power to bring people together to share in the human experience. It has been with us, evolving with us throughout time. Though highly variable, music is found in every known culture, past and present, and will most certainly be with us in the future. It is commonly believed that humans have been on the planet over 160,000 years and that music has been present for at least 50,000 years, and probably much longer than that. "Since all peoples of the world including the most isolated tribal groups, have a form of music, scientists conclude that music must have been present in the ancestral population prior to the dispersal of humans around the world." (Wallin, Brown, and Merker) Music quickly evolved to become a fundamental part of human life and has remained an integral part of human development, evolution, socialization and interaction.

Since music is such an ancient practice, there is no way of knowing exactly how long it's been with us or exactly how it all began, though my personal take is that since humans existed, music has existed and nature likely provided many of the inspirations, sounds, rhythm patterns and melodies that became the backbone of ancient music. It just makes sense. It's almost an innate thing to copy the sounds of nature: the bird whistles, we whistle back, the frog croaks we croak back, the coyote calls, and we want to call back! In Hawaii on the big island near Kona, where I was staying with my friend Morgan while writing this book, there was an incredibly rich sound-scape that took me into a deep altered state of consciousness every night. It became such a powerful experience to lay down every night and just surrender to the music of the jungle and watch the patterns that it brought forth in my mind's eye. Invariably, rhythms emerged in the night, and have become now part of me. Coqui frogs, ocean waves, the wind, and rain, birds and crickets all interweaving throughout the day and night created a constant musical backdrop for life in every moment. Considering that the origin of music may stem from naturally occurring sounds and rhythms is not something that science needs to prove to know that it's possible, just go out into nature and listen, and you'll have a glimpse of it very quickly! Human music echoes the natural environment by using patterns, repetition and tonalities that are represented there. Even today, some cultures have certain parts of their music intending to imitate natural sounds, particularly in shamanistic cultures.

Since the beginning of time, the ancient cultures of the world, in Africa, Asia, India, Australia, Indonesia, Europe and North America, have used drumming, singing and dancing as ways to connect with each other, communicate, celebrate, mourn, pray to the spirits of their land and express their spiritual, cultural and political beliefs as well as to teach socialization skills such as courtship, sexual education and others. Still today, it is woven into the very fabric of life for many of these cultures.

"Music is highly functional in African ethnic life, accompanying childbirth, rites of passage, harvesting food, marriage, hunting, and even political activities." (Wikkapedia)

"The Music of India has a history spanning millennia and, developed over several eras, remains fundamental to the lives of Indians today as sources of religious inspiration, cultural expression and pure entertainment." (Wikkapedia)

"Music has formed an integral part of the social, cultural and ceremonial observances of Australian Aboriginal and Torres Strait Islander peoples, down through the millennia of their individual and collective histories to the present day. Music song and dance was, and is still today, a very important part of Aboriginal life and customs. They have songs for every occasion, hunting songs, funeral songs, gossip songs and songs of ancestors, landscapes, animals, seasons, myths and Dreamtime legends." (Aboriginalart.com)

"Native American music plays a vital role in history and education, with ceremonies and stories orally passing on ancestral customs to new generations. Native American ceremonial music is traditionally said to originate from deities or spirits, or from particularly respected individuals. Every aspect of song, dance and costuming shapes rituals, and each aspect informs about the makers, wearers and symbols important to the nation, tribe, village, clan, family, or individual." (Heth)

"For the Inuit of Canada, chanting and drumming served many purposes for maintaining connection between the people. The chants told hunting stories, relieved tension between rivals, talked about hardship, sad and happy events, spirituality, and were a form of sharing emotions with others. When different family groups got together, there was much joy and the drum dances became part of the festivities and in this way, they shared their lives." (O'Neill)

Singing, drumming and dancing are enjoyed by all cultures. They are a tangible form of sharing life with others. In many traditional cultures, the word for music includes dancing, and singing as well as the instruments. "The treatment of "music" and "dance" as separate art forms is a European idea. In many African languages there is no concept corresponding exactly to these terms. For example, in many Bantu languages, there is one concept that might be translated as "song" and another that covers both the semantic fields of the European concepts of "music" and "dance." So there is one word for both music and dance (the exact meaning of the concepts may differ from culture to culture). And, in Kiswahili, the word "ngoma" may be translated as "drum," "dance," "dance event," "dance celebration" or "music," depending on the context." (Wikkopedia) This is relative to other cultures as well, Kala is the art of music in the East and has three aspects: vocal, instrumental and the expression of movement. (Khan) In seeing music as more inclusive of all parts of itself, it becomes a much more whole expression and art form, and creates more equality amongst all those who share in it by validating all parts of the same equally.

In these more traditional cultures, music has been passed down from generation to generation as a doorway for healing, community sharing, initiations, rites of passage, and for the invocations or banishment of spirits to bring rain or prepare the land for harvests, as well as for entertainment and countless other purposes. Music is inseparable from life, and entire villages and communities will participate together in its creation and celebration, each in their own unique way.

Being such an ancient human connection, it is easy to see why music still, today, in the modern world, holds the intrigue, power and connectivity that it does. It allows us a way to be together that extends beyond the conscious mind, it is an abstract vibration that allows us to "feel" something deeper than words can express adequately. It would be the most rare of beings that has not been, at some point, somewhere, touched by the power of music. It resonates the strings of human connectivity and brings us together to celebrate, mourn and feel together the experience of life: a sad song makes us feel our tender hearts, a disco song makes us want to get down and funk around, and even a song in a foreign language can make us feel the emotive energy that it captures simply in the vibration of the music and the voice.

"Music can move us to the heights or depths of emotion. It can persuade us to buy something, or remind us of our first date. It can lift us out of depression when nothing else can. It can get us dancing to its beat. But the power of music goes much, much further. Indeed, music occupies more areas of our brain than language does--humans are a musical species."   Oliver Sacks

"As we experience music, be it folk or classical, Indian or Western, we invariably recall our individual life-experience. Ascending and descending scales reflect the ups and downs in one's life. Vertical structure in western music such as chord, counterpoint, etc. make us feel the collective support that comes to us in our lonely journey of life. Sudden twists and bends, surprises and novelties are also not lacking in music. All these reflect those surprises and shocks, agonies and ecstasies, thrills and traumas we have to face in our life-journey. Regular appearance and disappearance of notes or tunes remind us of those precious people who join us and leave us, leaving behind glorious memories. Yet, the overall continuity of notes or phrases despite all those twists, bends or changes reminds us to be always optimistic and to look forward to life with confidence and courage." (Sairam)

Why does music appeal to humanity so much? The whole of creation has its origin in sound and vibration. Music represents something greater than ourselves and reminds us of our core connection to life thru vibration. Hazrat Inyat Khan, in his book, *The Music of Life*, says, "Our sense of music, our attraction to music, shows that there is music in the depth of our being. Music is behind the working of the whole universe. Music is life itself." (p. 71) Go and sit in nature for even a little while, watch and listen, and you can begin to get a sense for this easily. Even in the city, rhythm, tone, and melodies are everywhere around you all the time. Sound is a constant presence in our life, and the organization of sounds into familiar or repetitive patterns can make music out of life in every moment. Nature uses music to communicate, birds use their songs, cats their meows, dogs their barks and whales their surreal songs under the seas. Music appeals to us as humans because we are an organized mass of rhythms and tones: just listen to your heart beat, your breath and your own voice and pattern of speaking and there you can find the music of your life, and how life is affecting you even. You'll recognize that the music of your being will shift depending on what you're surrounded by, your inner state of being-ness, and even what time of the day it is. In the early morning your heartbeat and voice may be distinctly different than in late afternoon or evening. Your music changes as you walk thru your day. It is a common belief that humans are born musical, and it is our choice, environment, culture and lifestyle that dictate how much of that innate gift we utilize or access. It's always there though, always able to be accessed if we want to!

Oliver Sacks says, "We humans are a musical species, just as we are a linguistic species." Significantly, it is anthropologists and not just music educators who note that music is an essentially human practice and is found not only in all places in the world, but also under all circumstances. Music is known to promote physical as well as mental health, and is widely used for therapy in many clinical and educational applications worldwide. It is commonly used to help relieve stress, promote wellness, enhance memory, improve communication skills, promote physical rehabilitation, and even to alleviate pain. The human system responds to music often when it won't respond to anything else. I've worked in Assisted Living Centers with patients who the nurses swore couldn't communicate or even function, some with Alzheimer's, some with serious brain damage from strokes, some just in their last days of life and tired and apathetic. Yet I saw them participating, getting the beat and becoming alive again in the presence of music, responding with their whole being, tapping their feet, smiling, and suddenly even connecting with others. It's almost automatic; the beat just gets people going. Music can get thru where sometimes no other form of expression can.

Music brings people together, it unifies in a way nothing else can, always has, always will. It is not then so hard to understand, considering the ability of music to unite people, and create lasting bonds that a culture's music is often the first "target" by a dominating or oppressing culture. We see evidence of this throughout history, and are still, today experiencing the results of the disempowerment of the world's music cultures from the African Slaves to the Priestess drumming traditions of Europe, Egypt and Mesopotamia. The profound disempowerment of traditional peoples music was far more serious than a limited musical matter; this disempowerment affected their whole lives, in as much as their music had been an integral part of their whole lives. (Aboriginalart.com) The tragedies of the losses here are far beyond our ability to fully comprehend, and may never be fully known. The losses we have experienced are personally a deep grieving for myself as well as many others I know who share a love of cultural indigenous music.

Fortunately, some have survived in some form. So strong was the need to stay connected thru music, that many of those groups of people found ways to continue their traditions, and adapt them to preserve some piece of their culture. Capoeira is a perfect example of this adaptation. Capoeira is an Afro-Brazilian blend of martial art, game, and culture created by enslaved Africans in Brazil during the 16th Century. (Caoeira/Wikkapedia) Participants form a circle and take turns playing instruments, singing, and sparring in pairs in the center of the circle. Capoeira emerged as a way to resist oppression, secretly practice their art, transmit culture, and lift the spirits of the people. Maculele is a close relative to this art form and had a more aggressive spirit of venting anger and frustrations for the enslaved people, using machetes and then later sticks as part of the "game."

"Another adaptation was Candombe which originally designated the music, dance, instrumentation, and locales of the eighteenth- and nineteenth-century social events of reconstituted African nations in Uruguay. Africans of similar origins recreated a sense of identity and community based on old principles and new realities. Although ceasing to exist as such with the demise of the African-born population at the end of the nineteenth century, the African nations and the candombe have continued to reinvent themselves in new guises based on old foundations and new realities. Candombe became a source of inspiration for artistic representation in painting, in popular and classical music and dance, and in the Uruguayan carnival. Candombe also became the foundation of contemporary Afro-Uruguayan self-expression and the key element of the national cultural identity by which Uruguayans celebrate their uniqueness. Thus, the presumably nonexistent Afro-Uruguayan population, which has always been hyper visible in cultural production, maintains obvious continuities of Afrogenic culture in a society that proclaims its European heritage, while characterizing itself by its African heritage." (Walker)

In addition, Afro-Bolivians are basing their newly rediscovered sense of identity around the Afrogenic musical and dance form Saya, which had been disappearing as a result of their increasing assimilation into the larger society. And they are using that cultural rallying point as a basis for both the recovery of their oral history, often transmitted in Saya lyrics, and for promoting community development. (Walker)

The Santeria Religion is another example where the enslaved tribal people were able to preserve significant elements of their tradition such as sacred drumming, dance, and trance states for deity communication via "possession" by disguising their gods, or "orishas," as Catholic saints. On some level Blues, Bluegrass, and Hip Hop all have elements of adapting a traditional style for survival in a new world. These forms are deeply significant in that they maintained a connection between people who shared some history, experiences and passion. The new forms disguised themselves in ways that their oppressors could be exposed to without feeling threatened; they adapted elements of their new environment's culture and wove them into the fabric of their older traditions. They also became forms of communication, in and of themselves, of the people, for the people, by the people, becoming "folk" traditions in essence.

Even today, these creative adaptations of sacred drum and dance, and many others that have emerged, continue to hold great power to unify people all over the world. Now, even people from other cultures and traditions are drawn to participating in the music and dances of these and other ancient peoples. I believe that there are many reasons for this, and that the primary draw is the experience of connectivity and sharing, learning and celebrating together thru music that these "folk" ways so strongly instills in those who participate. It is the human connection, beyond the music, beyond the form, that has allowed these practices to survive, and even thrive, thru the ages and it is the human connection in music that is what teaches us the most.

Music and Children:
Vital Connection for Healthy Socialization of our Youth

"Music students have an increased ability to assess their own work, give and receive criticism, articulate goals, approach their work in an ideal, engaging way, work independently and with others, and draw upon available resources. What enviable qualities to have in a community and its work force! We also know that the benefits of music programs spill over into the non-music classes. Answer that, budget-cutters!" (Orford)

"We attach supreme importance to a musical education, because rhythm and harmony sink most deeply into the recesses of the soul and take most powerful hold of it, bringing gracefulness, health and wellbeing in their wake." (Orford)

There is no disputing the significance of music education for our youth to learn invaluable life skills. Research in music education clearly shows, time and time again, the undeniable significance of music in education and in the development of a young person's mind and learning, relating and communicating abilities. Even in the United States, music has, for the most part, been identified as a core subject in the education system. While there have most certainly been huge cutbacks in funding for schools educational programs in music and the arts (see next chapter for more), there is also a very strong contingent operating towards supporting music in schools, as the evidence is so strong in favor of music making for better citizens and more complete beings as adults. The U.S. House of Representatives unanimously passed House Concurrent Resolution 121, on April 26, 2007, recognizing the benefits of school-based music education. This resolution states, "that it is the sense of the Congress that music education grounded in rigorous instruction is an important component of a well-rounded academic curriculum and should be available to every student in every school." Twenty-five representatives co-sponsored the bill. This represents a shift for the US, as music education programs have been hard hit and under funded in the past 10 years. The resolution states "music enhances skills necessary for the 21st century," including "the ability to analyze, solve problems, communicate, and work cooperatively." Children who do not have music education in their school are "at a disadvantage compared to their peers in other communities." Further, it points out that children involved in music are "less likely to be involved with drugs, gangs, or alcohol and have better attendance in school." (Schoolmusicmatters.com)

Some of the other well documented and well-known benefits of music education for children, amongst others, are as follow:

1. Development of language and reasoning faculties in the brain
Early musical training helps develop brain areas involved in language and reasoning. It is thought that brain development continues for many years after birth. Recent studies have clearly indicated that musical training physically develops the part of the left side of the brain known to be involved with processing language, and can actually wire the brain's circuits in specific ways.

2. Improvements in spatial and temporal intelligence/reasoning
A causal link between music and spatial intelligence (the ability to perceive the world accurately and to form mental pictures of things) has been discovered repeatedly in music education research. This kind of intelligence helps one to visualize various elements that should go together, and is critical to basic common sense thinking that is necessary for everything from solving advanced mathematics problems to being able to plan out a day's needs for school or work.

3. Improved capacity for problem solving and creative thinking
Music and art students learn to think creatively and to solve problems by imagining various solutions. Musical "solutions" can have more than one "right" answer and so create pathways to think creatively and explore several options or solutions to the same concern or problem. This has limitless applications for real life skills of dealing with conflicts, problems and life experiences.

4. Increase in test scores and Overall Improved academic performance
Repeated studies have shown that students who study music are more successful on standardized tests such as the SAT. They also achieve higher grades in high school overall and are more involved in the academic experience.

5. Enhanced Tolerance for Diversity, and Global Consciousness
A diverse and well-approached musical education provides children with a unique lens to experience the diversity of other cultures. It

offers an opportunity to generate a sense of the bigger world we live in, and also to develop empathy, compassion and respect for other cultures, thus providing a bridge across cultural chasms. When children are exposed to this concept at a young age, it helps to create a more culturally diverse and tolerant future for generations to come.

6. Increased math and science comprehension/performance

Many studies have proven that music skills increase students' performance abilities, test scores and comprehension of math, and the sciences. The skills learned in music are directly connected to the processes needed for the kind of rational thought that math and science require.

7. Increased Immune Response

A child's saliva tested before and after a 30-minute music session interacting with simple, recognizable tunes, showed heightened immunoglobulin (a key indicator of the immune system) after the session vs. kids with no music session. There have been several documented cases of immune response increasing with exposure to playing music or listening to music in adults as well as children.

8. Development of Discipline and Teamwork Skills

Music study enhances teamwork skills and discipline. In order for an orchestra to sound good, all players must work together harmoniously towards a single goal, and must commit to learning music, attending rehearsals, and practicing. Learning to work together as a team for a common purpose teaches a deep understanding of community building skills and give and take. Discipline fosters also a sense of accomplishment, and a conscious understanding of the rewards of disciplined application of the mind.

9. Increased Self-Expression and Communication Skills

Music provides children with a means of self-expression. Self-esteem is a natural by-product of this self-expression. Children that are able to express themselves will in turn be more prepared and capable of communicating their needs and listening to others. Music teaches listening as one of the primary tools for effective communication.

10. Increased Participation In Life

Music study develops skills that are necessary in the workplace; many of the above are relative to having a successful work life as well as personal life. Music is an active process, it encourages active participation and not just observation, and it encourages active engagement with all levels of being. Employers today are looking for multi-dimensional workers with the sort of flexible and supple intellects that music education helps to create as described above.

11. Decreases drop out rates for at risk students

At risk students, when given the opportunity to get involved in an arts program have a much higher likelihood of finishing school. Music and the arts contribute to lower recidivism rates, increased self-esteem, the acquisition of job skills, and the development of much needed creative thinking, problem solving and communications skills in at risk youth. In short, research shows that music education helps them to develop as contributing members of society. In addition, their academic performance improves significantly. It gives them a sense of personal expression, and instills a community awareness where they can participate with others and feel validated and feel a part of something. It also provides a place to channel their energy that is constructive and creative instead of destructive.

12. Development of Motor Skills

The physical benefits of early childhood music are obvious! Handling the instrument, and/or dance improve fine and gross motor skills, and listening and singing are great reinforcements for improving speech and vocal development!

13. Increased Success in the Workplace

Mastery of the arts has been shown to be just as closely correlated with high earnings as those with technical or computer mastery. In "The Paradox of the Silicon Savior" Grant Venerable reported, "The very best engineers and technical designers in the Silicon Valley industry are, nearly without exception, practicing musicians." Many large corporations and companies are using music making now as part of their strategies to teach valuable skills for business. Adults who were educated musically as children will come to the table with those skills already somewhat developed.

Music gives life meaning, and in our fast paced modern world, music remains as a fixed point of reference in an unpredictable world, something we can always return to for solace, connection, and medicine. Children who are exposed to music making opportunities are more apt to be better integrated in every way when they mature into adults. They will naturally understand that their part matters in the whole, as music teaches the interdependence of one part on another.

Merging Flesh with Spirit: Divine Human Connection

"The mystics of all ages have loved music most. In almost all religions around the world, music seems to be the center of the ceremony. Those who attain to that perfect peace called nirvana, do this more easily through music." (Khan, p. 121)

In addition to providing the human-to-human connection that is necessary for a whole well being to participate in society, culture and the family unit, music also provides direct access to the Divine, or to our "higher" selves. Many of the bards and musicians of the world have been recognized as holy people, priests, priestesses and sages. There is a profound wisdom that music teaches that allows us to transcend the mundane and the physical.

"All spiritualists who have really sounded the depths of spiritualism have realized that there is no better means of attracting the spirits from their plane of freedom to the outer plane than by music. There is no magic like music for making an effect upon the human soul." (Khan, p. 52) I often use the term "the human instrument" in my groups and meditations. The human instrument is perfectly created to allow for the flow of cosmic energies as well as earthly energies. It is unique in that it can not only echo the natural environment but can also pull from the inner soundscapes, personality and even the cosmos to create music. Playing music or "channeling" music, helps to shift the consciousness to a more receptive state, an altered state even. Science has proven what the mystics have known for eons, that there is an actual change in the activity of the brain to a different state of consciousness. There are many books written on this undeniable reality, most recently Daniel Levitin, "This is your Brain on Music" and "Musicophilia" by Oliver Sacks, so I won't be going in depth here to re-create work that has already been so well done. Those books are both definitely worth a read to gain a deeper understanding of the science of this natural phenomenon of music and the human instrument.

Threads in the Fabric of Life

A few years ago, I was traveling in India for almost 2 months. I was so deeply and constantly touched by the reverence of the people in their music, dance and spiritual practices. Everywhere there was music, people singing and dancing, prayer and ritual and more music. It felt really like one big community everywhere I traveled in India, unified mostly thru the people's music, the songs, the rhythms and the devotion and appreciation for life. I felt more at home there, in that foreign world than I ever did in my own hometown in Florida. Somehow, they valued what I valued: human connection, God, music and service, and I was accepted unquestionably as a part of the whole fabric of life. Their way of life made more sense to me right away than my own culture has after a lifetime of contemplation and observation.

I stayed for almost 4 weeks in a village called Omkaweshwar, and there experienced some of the most profound music and devotional spirit I've ever experienced. This village felt like it was still very in connection with its roots. It felt like it had yet to be corrupted or polluted too much by the western mentalities, though it was easy to see it was creeping in more and more thru the TV's racy images and the newest addition to the town, the internet café. It was the only place I went in India where I was charged the same prices as the locals, so that definitely said something to me. The concept of greed hadn't overcome the people and the connection of human to human was still overriding any differences in nationalities or background. I found that to be the case in all my experiences there. The deeper part of their culture was so prevalent, so in my face every day, and always warmly inviting me to participate.

My first day there, as I was walking down the street I heard drumming resonating down the alleyways. I recognized the sound of the dholak, and was instantly interested to see what was happening. Peeking into the building where the music was coming from, I was sweetly surprised to see a strong elder woman, probably in her mid 50's, playing a drum with such power, such shakti, and such grace that I was fully captivated. Her voice was profound, it held a human quality that was intangible, holding all the pain, suffering, joy and gratitude that I know to be part of the human experience and then some. She was a true diva of the drum, and the power that she hit the drum with was the same power I've felt in my own hands. I could recognize it effortlessly and almost instantly tears came to my eyes when I saw her there. Here in this foreign place, this ancient town on a Holy River, she was reflecting a part of myself to me. Around her were seated about 50 women, all dressed in sari's, singing in response to her calls, many of them fully veiled and in a state of trance swaying back and forth. One of the women saw me and motioned for me to come in, and I did. Closing my eyes, in that circle of women, I was transported to another place and time. I remembered a deep part of myself, felt a connection beyond anything I could verbally express and felt tears of gratitude for the experience flowing freely.

One of the women saw me, and she must have really seen me beyond my pale skin and western heritage, because she handed me a drum with a look of knowingness, like she knew I could play and that I wanted to play. I played with this elder woman of the drum with tears streaming wildly down my face, sharing in the Shakti of Rhythm with my sister whom I loved dearly though had just met. When she heard my hands hit the drum, matching her own power and grace, she too shed a tear, and we nodded in total acknowledgement of equals meeting from different worlds. I had the opportunity to listen and play with her several times while I was there, and though we weren't able to really talk, as we couldn't speak each other's languages, we shared in something deeper than words can reflect, a kinship and a knowingness that the other exists, a deep mutual respect and appreciation, and some intangible bond was created that I know will exist for the eons of time until we meet again.

That entire month I was in Omkaweshwar, no matter what time of day or night, when I heard her strike the drum or sing a note, I knew instantly it was she. None of the other women held quite the same intensity of connection, the depth of feeling that she did, though many of them sang beautifully. Often it was in the middle of the night, as they often played from 12 am till 3 or 4 am in temples or old buildings. When I heard her, I was drawn, like a moth to a flame, and would get up out of a deep sleep to go and witness this amazing sharing of women in rhythm. They were Gujarat women and I deeply honored that they were holding on to a sacred practice that had been part of their culture for many generations.

That whole month, every day was a surreal musical experience: in the early morning the monks were chanting and playing gongs and bells in the most ethereal melodies imaginable, across the river songs and chants floated, and often in the middle of the night a parade of drummers would come thru the middle of the village wildly celebrating a marriage or some other community occurrence. Music was life, life was music, everywhere, every day. There wasn't a concept of "going to see" music, it just was there all the time, surrounding life, an inevitable part of life, weaving one moment into the next. It always felt natural and effortless, like it just flowed thru the entire village all the time and each person there was somehow a part of it.

In India, I daily got a giggle out of the thought that in the US, if drummers came drumming and singing down the street celebrating a marriage in the middle of the night, someone would call the police and make a noise complaint or cry that it was too loud or complain that they'd been "disturbed." In India, and in other cultures around the world, no one even bats an eye, they wake up, and feel happy that someone is getting married. They are celebrating life in their hearts too, or if they're unhappy about it, they just suck it up and go back to sleep. There doesn't even seem to be a consideration of calling the police to complain about music.

In the western world, music has become increasingly separate from daily life. It isn't woven into the fabric of our daily life in the same way that it once was and still is in traditional cultures. Not to say that people aren't listening to music, buying and downloading music, etc. but more that music has been "sold" to us as much more of a spectator sport than a participatory community experience. Sadly, it is often discouraged more than encouraged, and often even considered "noise." I know of many people personally who say they'd play more if they had a space, but they can't because of a neighbor or a roommate being "not into it." Someone practicing in their own living room even can be considered a "disturbance," and acoustic live music on the streets is forbidden in many towns, neighborhoods and cities. House concerts are becoming more difficult to do these days, and now often permits are required just to invite people over to listen to music in one's own home. It's ludicrous really how much control there is over how, when, and what kind of music is "permissible" in mainstream culture.

Noise complaints about music are really an interesting phenomenon to me: I have always found it fascinating that weed whackers, lawn mowers or jackhammers never get a "noise complaint" but music so often will, whether it's in the city streets, or in the privacy of a home. I'm constantly amazed at this, and of course there are exceptions, but in many communities in our culture, people have to rent out specific spaces, or play within certain hours of the day to not be "disturbing" to others and to avoid dealing with noise complaints and angry neighbors, etc. I understand the need for quiet time, and respect that, yet it just doesn't seem to be that there is a fair reciprocity of allowance for the need for music as a basic human experience. Perhaps it is worthy of consideration that allowing for quiet, and allowing for music could be equal considerations and a basic acceptance between people rather than some point of contention. Perhaps we ought to create a "Disturbing the Music" ordinance where we can be entitled to making music in our homes just as equally as our neighbors are entitled to their constant quiet. It's just not a balanced equation. Try to have a gathering where people are drumming and singing the way those women in India did, or just have a small party in the back yard and have a few people strumming, drumming and singing songs together, and see what happens. Unless you're way out somewhere with no neighbors, or you're really blessed to have musical neighbors (which I hope is the case for all of us someday) chances are you'll get a nasty phone call, or a rap on your door from a police officer for "disturbing the peace." Things have to be quiet after 9 or 10 PM, which is the prime time for play for music lovers, and some of the best times to unwind into the depths of music's ecstasy as well as the best creative hours. The nighttime is the right time and for people working full days, it is the only time available in their lives to gather, celebrate, and share in the passion of music! I offer my gratitude for the tolerant amongst us who can see the value and community spirit that music brings to a home, family and community and delight and celebrate in a neighbors party or music rather than being "bothered" by it!

Imagine if people turned off their TV's and computers, and instead gathered and played music at night or even just got together to share stories and listen to music to relax and unwind. There was once such a time and some of the best music and deepest connections have come from those times! Imagine if we unplugged from the concept that other people's lives thru sitcoms or reality shows, media, etc. are more interesting than our own by tuning into the channel of here and now! Imagine if we took part in creating the comedy and resolving the drama in our own lives instead of just watching people on TV do it! Several years ago, when I was in college, a friend came to my room and was amazed that I didn't have a TV. "What do you do?" he asked me, seriously amazed that I didn't own a TV. I was equally as amazed with the question! Life in and of itself, for me, is a constant show, a constant source of wonder, amazement and spontaneity, a constant opportunity to witness the unfolding of a mystery and I get to play a part in writing the script in each moment! Why would I want a TV to distract me from the magic unfolding before me?

Imagine the possibilities of unplugging, even partially from the modern mainstream media machines. We would have a social revolution as people learned to be together again, to honor the expression, the pain and the joys of life together, to create their own "shows" instead of watching other people's lives and then feeling "inadequate" in context to the "stars" on TV, or worse, trying to be like them or look like them. If we all stepped into being the stars of our own lives, singing it, dancing it, and sharing it with our communities, inevitably the world around us would begin to shift and the consciousness of our culture would slowly, but surely follow suit. We all have stories to tell, and by sharing them we gain the wisdom of each other, and become more capable to deal with our "stuff" thru the witnessing of each other's trials and victories in life shared.

Music holds tremendous ability and power for human connection to happen because it allows us a vehicle to connect in non-verbal ways that touch upon the parts of life experience that are intangible and unable to be fully described in words alone. It also holds the connection between the human vessel and the Divine, and those who participate can easily access other realms thru its magical portals. Music is the language of emotion, and captures our emotions in ways that words simply cannot. Add words to the emotion, and the quality of the voice emerges thru it to add the elements of mysticism and embodiment and we have a true merging of spirit with flesh: music as life through the human instrument.

Chapter 3

Music:
By the People
For the People

"Folk music is like an un-weeded bio-reserve. Who can deny its down-to-earth robustness, the verve, vigor and vitality which is closer to nature and presented in a more truthful manner than modern music."
Author Unknown

Music is such a vast human experience with so many aspects to be considered. Saying music is a universal language is true, and yet different forms of music evoke different responses in us, and each form has it's own "dialect" or "tongue." So, in essence, it's just like our world. We all can experience the "human" experience, but each culture has it's own expression of that and it's own unique manifestations of life based on it's unique factors. These factors include, but are not limited to social, economic, environmental, ancestoral, and traditional. I see music very much like I see the many cultures of this planet: all are intrinsically valuable and have something to teach us, all have a place and a time of their own, and all forms of music offer something unique and irreplaceable as expressions of life and the greater cosmic creation we are a part of.

In primitive traditional cultures there were members of the tribe who specialized in carrying the music forth. It was their job to maintain the oral traditions, songs, dances and stories of their people, with their people, yet it is also true that everyone participated in the experience musically. In Africa, the term "Griot" is still used today. A griot is a praise singer, or a wandering musician, considered a repository of oral tradition. Griots carry an ancestoral responsibility that follows a blood line to ensure the survival of the music in a pure form. This is seen in many other traditions: in the Celtic world, the term "bard" was used, or "minstrel." In India, the "udgatr" was the chanter of melodies, in Ancient Greece, in the fourth and fifth centuries BC and perhaps earlier, a "rhapsode" was a professional performer of poetry. The "sage" had a similar role as did the "Mystic" and the "Muse." These were the closest things to what we now consider "Professionals" in the Muse Arts: music, dance, poetry, storytelling, etc.

Their lives were/are dedicated to learning the stories, songs and traditions of their people, most of which has been and still is passed down orally. They wore many hats: they were entertainment, they channeled the spirit world, and they were responsible for performing at rituals, rites of passage and other community happenings. They carried the wisdom of generations in their musical expressions. These individuals held a great role in their communities, and were valued as important people in the community. They were treated with respect for their dedication and path, but they were not deemed "special," in the way the western mind often glamorizes the musician. People didn't think of music as some special talent per se, it was simply recognized that they were either born into that tradition, or chose it out of desire. Music was something everyone could and did do, some just more than others and some as more of a life path than others.

"To western minds, music is generally considered to be a rare talent possessed only by a few. As a consequence, most contemporary thinkers who have pondered the evolutionary contribution of music to human life regard it as an enexplicable "mystery" because it is so unevenly distributed among individuals. (Barrow, 1995). If one looks at traditional societies, however, it is evident that music is as broadly endowed as any other human capacity, and virtually everyone participates in music making. Differences in performing and composing ability are attributed to differences in individual interest and desire, not to special endowment. (Feld, 1984:390)." (Brown and Volgesten)

There is a tremendous amount of research that explores the concept of "talent" vs. "acquired skill" and it repeatedly shows that talent isn't necessarily a true concept. "Talent" is defined as a genetic propensity or something "special" in the development of the brain. Traditional cultures realize that we are all musical beings, but the western mind is sadly still living in this thought process that musicians, artists, and dancers are born, not crafted. Musicologists and cognitive scientists have studied expertise for over three decades. "In almost all cases, musical expertise has been defined as technical achievement."(Levitin p. 194) In other words: practice! People who become more musically proficient simply practice more, they have more commitment to it, they want to learn, and so spend countless hours working, learning and practicing. The practice does in fact increase the size of that part of the brain that is used for the practice, but it has not been discovered that it happens the other way around. Considering a healthy normal child, we are all born with equal potential to music!

In today's modern world a musician is defined as a person who plays music or composes music. Sometimes the term can include other people who produce music such as:

* A vocalist who uses his or her voice as an instrument.
* Composers and songwriters who write music.
* A conductor who coordinates a musical ensemble.

The concept of the musician and the status of the musician in society varies from culture to culture. Both singer and instrumentalist can be improvisers, who create new music in real time. Musicians can be either amateur or professional. Professional musicians are paid musicians who use performing as their main source of income. They may work freelance, enter into a contract with a studio or record label, be employed by a professional ensemble such as a symphony orchestra, or be employed by an institution such as a church or business (such as a bar). Musicians usually attempt to attain a high level of proficiency, constantly practicing to develop the skills needed to perform their chosen style. For example, the practice of scales and modes by Instrumentalists."(Wikkopedia)

However, it is not at all true or accurate to say that *only* professional or trained musicians can play and enjoy making music, nor is it true that only those who have studied music can appreciate the deep human connection that music fosters within. "Many of our greatest musical minds weren't considered experts in a technical sense." (Levitin) Certainly not everyone has the desire, time or ability to spend their lives studying music at the level that trained or classical musicians will, as traditional cultures recognized and honored. Yet still many non-musicians are called to be in the presence of music, to listen, to dance, to celebrate and to connect in musical environments.

The most basic elements of music, rhythm and melody, can be felt and recognized by anyone, musician or not. "In music, the thing that matters is whether you feel it or not. You can't intellectualize music; to reduce it analytically often is to reduce it to nothing very important." (Coleman,1960) (Farmelo) Traditional cultures used rhythm and voice as their two primary instruments, and from this foundation created complex songs that an entire village of people would know and participate in. Even today, many folk traditions are still alive in their essence thru the rhythm and the melody of songs passed down thru ordinary, every day people creating music that is truly by the people, for the people: generation after generation.

Folk music, in the most basic sense of the term, is music by and from the common people. The Sally Bingham Center for Women's Culture defines it as "music of culturally homogeneous people without formal training, generally according to regional customs and continued by oral traditions." The Tech Multimedia Music Dictionary defines it as "music of the common people that has been passed on by memorization or repetition rather than by writing, and has deep roots in its own culture." Where folk music is still surviving, it is still being passed on in this way today. According to Webster's dictionary, folk music is the "traditional and typically anonymous music that is an expression of the life of the people in a community."

In particular, what distinguishes folk music is that it is participatory. People play and sing together rather than watching others perform. Another interesting aspect of folk music is that it often emerges spontaneously from communities of ordinary people. Finally, and perhaps most significantly, it brings a sense of community and a basic experience of human connection. It is the people's music, and irreplaceable as a way of bringing everyday people together to share the experience of life.

Folk music has taken many forms throughout history from the tribal cultures' songs, dances and rituals, to today's folk rock musicians or singer/songwriter artists such as Bob Dylan and Joan Baez. Ragtime, swing, bluegrass and mountain music fit into this category, as well as Irish, Celtic and most forms of World Music which all have some root in older more traditional cultures.

The Suppression of Tribal Music

Traditional or tribal folk is considered the oldest form of music. Instruments were basic: simple and rhythmical in nature. Drums, rattles, bells, flutes and voice formed the musical foundations and were for many centuries the only instruments used. The drum has been well documented to be one of the very first, if not *the* first, musical instrument other than the human voice. It's connection has always been an integral part of music as the pulse. The primordial rhythm that creates and sustains life is able to be echoed thru human hands when playing a drum. The drumming aspect of traditional cultures was also always a mysterious and sometimes haunting experience for the early explorers from the western world.

In the late 1800's, Europeans first encountering tribal music, were deeply touched and shared fascinating stories in their memoirs as the following excerpt from memoirs collected in the late 1800's demonstrates in regards to African tribal music.

"Other travellers, too, who have heard them have spoken of them in terms of high praise, Burchell even going so far as to declare that mere words were insufficient to describe their beauties. "They must be heard; they must be participated in." From these dances he derived as much pleasure as did the natives, so quiet and orderly were they. No rude laughter, no noisy shouting, no coarse, drunken, ribald wit was there; throughout it was a modest, sociable amusement. Music softened all their passions, and thus they lulled themselves into that mild and tranquil state in which no evil thoughts approach the mind. The soft and delicate voices of the girls, instinctively accordant to those of the women and the men, the gentle clapping of the hands, the rattles of the dancers, and the mellow sound of the water-drum, all harmoniously attuned and keeping time together, the peaceful happy countenances of the party, and the cheerful light of the fire, were circumstances so combined and fitted to produce the most soothing effects on the senses, that I sat as if the hut had been my home, and felt as though I had been one of them."(Wallaschek)

I feel this story really captures the undeniable pull that these most ancient forms of "folk" music exert on the human spirit, and the feeling of unity that this way of sharing naturally creates within us. In spite of the Europeans arrogance and persecution of these same people, they couldn't help but be caught up when they really allowed themselves to experience the music.

Of course, this wasn't the experience had by many of the Europeans when first encountering the "old" worlds where traditional people's used the drum as part of their ritual and music. For the most part, unfortunately, the Europeans were terrified of drumming, dancing and singing around fires, as there was nothing quite like it where they came from in the "civilized" world. They considered it primitive and there are just as many stories criticizing and denigrating the music of ancient peoples. Many related it to witchcraft and other "pagan" religions, which were highly persecuted by the Roman Empire as early as the 4th century. Most of the early explorers could only relate to the tribal customs as threatening and hostile, because they had no real context, education, or awareness of the truth of what the music was conveying or the purpose it served to unite the people. They were fearful people gravely trespassing on land they were seeking to dominate, and most were convinced of their "rightness" thus, consequently, the "wrongness" of anything different. In that ignorance those early explorers wreaked havoc everywhere they touched ground, all over this planet. They took from the world immeasurable amounts of deep wisdom, mysticism, music, countless lives, ancestoral knowledge, traditions and possibilities we will never be able to fully account for. This is a well known and well documented tragedy that has been repeated far too many times around the world. Fortunately, these stories are being told more and more now, and slowly what is left is returning and being honored again now in the hearts and minds of many modern people around the world. Efforts are now being made at preserving and recording what remains and protecting it so that it lives on in some way. The respect for these ways is returning as we come full circle and recognize what we have lost.

As discussed previously, these ravaged cultures adapted as much as they could to preserve aspects of their heritage, and some, particularly in India, Asia, Africa and the Middle East, are still in survival today in spite of their contact with Europeans. This to me is a miracle and a gift that I pray is preserved and maintained as long as humans exist. In addition, what did survive thru adaptation has managed to filter into the Western culture and has kept, at least to some degree, a connection to the roots of the tradition.

For many years, even into modern times, due to the fearful misconceptions that were prevalent for generations, drumming and dancing were considered "demonic," "satanic," and "savage." Those who chose to participate did so in private, and often fearing for their lives. Personal friends of mine, elders in the pagan/shaman communities now, have shared with me that even in their lifetimes, 20-40 years ago, they didn't dare mention that they drummed and danced, much less around a fire, for fear of repercussions, police investigation or being outcast from their communities, many of which were Christian or Catholic. Some of them were raised by parents who had roots or interests in the Old World religions, and traditions, and spoke of the fear their parents lived with even in a country where there was supposed to be "religious tolerance" and "freedom of speech."

One woman I know, who is now in her 60's, was one of the few women who dared to tread into the very much male dominated world of drumming in the 1960's and 1970's. She was also learning about her roots, which were from the Yoruba people of Africa. In her mind, because she was studying the religion and traditions of that culture, her *ancestoral heritage,* and because she wasn't a devout Christian, she was heavily persecuted. She told me one night after a good groove session, that she was often called a witch, and threatened, to the point that she had to leave the community she grew up in, in Georgia, to escape the harassement. She learned to be very quiet about it until much later in her life, when it became more socially acceptable.

The deep influence of the Salem Witch trials, and the overall mis-perception of the Pagan, or Earth based religions, from tribal peoples, to the Goddess worshipping cultures of Europe, Egypt and Mesopotamia, cast a fearful shadow over any activity that even remotely resembled these ways. Drumming and dancing, around a fire in particular, were deemed "bad," by mainstream culture in general for many years and in particular by certain fear based religions and sects of people. Even today, in the modern world, there is a great lack of awareness around these sub-cultures. Fortunately, some of that is changing now with drum circles now being used in corporate settings, schools, and churches (yes even Christian ones). In addition, the information era is providing us with more accurate information about people, customs and belief systems from the past, thus unveiling more truth in the mysteries of the histories of peoples, tribes and religions.

The drum holds a very unique doorway to musical participation. Few other instruments can provide such easy access to those who have not studied music as a life path but still want to participate and be involved. As the first instrument, resonating the sound of creation, the pulse of the cosmos and the heartbeat of humanity, the drum anchors us to earthly existence, while simultaneously providing a platform for altered states of consciousness, shamanistic journey work, heightened, prolonged states of ectasy and transformational possibilities. Most importantly for western culture it is a very accessible way to begin to connect musically with others. Since rhythm is the most basic element of musical expression, it allows for an accessible opportunity for people to begin the process and journey of musical expression. As the foundational piece for music, it also provides the framework for other forms of expression such as song, dance, other instruments, spoken word, and all forms of the Muse.

The drum circle as it is commonly referred to today is an adaptation of a traditional practice that is worthy of recognition. In the western world, it has birthed it's own "folk" tradition here that satisfies and fits the classical definition perfectly. Each group has it's own unique voicing, and expression based on the members, their backgrounds, and experiences. The drum circle is a place where people can express themselves in the company of others. It holds the potential to model equality as it includes people of all ages, faiths and ethnicities. The main objective of an open community circle is to share rhythm and entrain, or connect to each other. It invites and includes everyone and does not necessarily require any previous knowledge or skill Drumming, dancing and being together in this old way holds great potential to help unify us and create a remembrance of sharing ourselves thru music.

It is music truly for the people, by the people.

Chapter 4

The Glamorization
of Popular Music
and
The Decline of Music Making

"If the USA is any guide to what is happening in the rest of the industrialized world, more and more people are doing less and less music making for themselves, year by year from around 1927 to the present. We need to persuade our fellow artists and humanists that there is a critical loss of music making going on that is not 'natural' or 'inevitable' nor is it natural that just the 'talented' few are doing something and the 'untalented' many are applauding, as usual." (Keil)

"An article written in 2004, "The Unprecedented Decline of Music Education in California Public Schools" unveiled a 50 percent decline in the percentage of students in music education programs from 1999-2004, representing an actual student loss of over one-half million students. During this same period the total California public school student population increased by 5.8%. This decline is the largest of any academic subject area." (www.futureofmusic.org)

As a society, we are taught that we "Go and see" music, that there is an "appropriate" place to "go and see" music (bars, nightclubs, etc.), and that we have to "pay" to see people "perform" or "pay" to have lessons for the priveledge of learning. The free sharing of information that happens in more traditional cultures with music, the passing on, generation to generation of rhythms, songs, dances and musical etiquette, just isn't prevalent in western culture. Music has seen a progression, over time, of commercial interests. Again here we have "need and greed," on the part of artists, the "industry," corporations; and the seemingly always present concept of the western mindset that everything has a price and can be bought and/or sold. Music and the arts have suffered tremendously from this way of being. It has shifted the consciousness of creativity from one of a playful exploratory child to a business man making deals for big bucks.

Prior to the 20th century, the concept of selling music wasn't really commonplace. One of the very first to consider music as a marketable commodity was Wolfgang Amadeus Mozart. "In the mid-to-late 1700s, performers and composers such as Wolfgang Amadeus Mozart began to seek commercial opportunities to market their music and performances to the general public." (Wikkapedia /Dear Constanze The Guardian) Before that, in more traditional cultures, the Griots, bards, and musicians were cared for by their communities, as equals in the tribe doing their part to contribute. In Europe, up until the 1700's music was supported by patronage from the aristocracy, or the church, and so there was no need for artists to sell themselves; and so the concept of selling music had just not yet come to be.

A crucial change in the history of folk music began during the twentieth century with folk artists adopting the very western concept of "marketing for money," or "selling" the music of the people. In this time, a new genre of popular music arose that basically became an imitation of the original traditions of folk music as it was sung by ordinary people. These "folk" artists marketed themselves alongside more popular and modern emerging artists and created a niche for themselves by performing traditional music and songs in amplified concerts, and disseminating their work by recordings and broadcasting. Such artists included Pete Seeger, Burl Ives, Jimmie Rodgers and Woody Guthrie who began by singing songs his mother had sung to him as a child. Also are performers such as Bob Dylan, Joan Baez and Joni Mitchell, all of whom took folk to new levels by writing music that represented the feelings of the people of their times. Folk Rock came about and folk, as a popular genre quickly evolved to be quite different than its original roots, creating a form of music that shifted the experience from it's original essence of participatory to more of a spectator experience, as the original older songs were forgotten and the idea of capitalizing on folk songs became firmly rooted. (Wikkapedia)

Also in the 20th Century, the "Extravaganza" arose which was a form of lavish and elaborate theater. The shows were considered sexually titillating, with women singing bawdy songs dressed in nearly transparent clothing and were widely criticized by the media and churches of the day. David Ewen described this as the beginning of the "long and active careers in sex exploitation of American musical theater and popular song." This new genre also was emerging at the same time that what I call the "Glamorization" of music and musicians was emerging. To glamorize means to make something seem more interesting, romantic or desirable than it really is, or to "hype" it up beyond itself. It was during this time that people began to idolize artists. Physical appearance, sex appeal and "star" qualities began to be as, or more, significant than musicality or skill. This was a new and very western concept. Music was suddenly related to "star" quality or a "special talent," and sex appeal This is something worthy of noting. I actually had a producer tell me in 2000 that if I wanted to make it in the music biz I needed to remember that "sex sells" and I should dress sexier and use that edge more, and that my talent mattered less than my look. Music is a basic human potentiality, a natural occurrence in the human species, as we've looked at in chapter 2 and can come thru all shapes, sizes, and forms with equanimity and variance. Music has nothing to do with sex appeal or glamour but, indeed, the westernized concept of music made it so!

The middle of the 20th century saw a number of very important changes in American popular music. The field of pop music developed tremendously during this period. The increasingly low price of recorded music stimulated demand and also much greater profits for the record industry. As a result, music marketing became more and more prominent. Music and money have now become deeply intertwined in a fascinating dance of commercialization, greed, exploitation of artists, and glamorization. In and of itself, the exchange of music for money holds no good or bad implication for me and I am not in any way arguing for or against that exchange. As a recording artist myself, I completely get and validate the artistic and creative process of crafting a song or an album and being compensated for that by others who may appreciate, resonate or be inspired by it. I know the amount of dedication, work and devotion that goes into crafting a song and am fully in support of artists being supported and compensated for their contributions!

In addition, I do feel deeply that it is important to remember that music is for everyone! That it is a crucial part of the human dance offering invaluable community building opportunities, socialization skills and human bonding. When we overvalue one type of music (modern, popular, commercial) and undervalue any other we create an imbalance in the natural essence of music. The heart and soul of music is about coming together, sharing, expressing and feeling our connectivity. When that gets lost to the almighty dollar, the big crowds and the game of it all, and forgotten or even pushed aside for financial gain, music becomes almost unnatural, and loses some piece of it's inherent magic.

It is difficult to really imagine now, for many of us, that there was a time when music wasn't a commodity, a specialized "skill" or a game of money. There was a time, and it still exists in some folk and tribal communities, that music was simply for the sake of music, a way of life and a part of life. It wasn't relative if you had a "look" or not, or how much you could turn on the opposite sex. It didn't matter what kind of clothes you wore or who you "knew." You didn't need to know every mode, scale or methodology to be an active participant. Whatever piece you felt to contribute: dance, story, song, drumming, was equally valued and appreciated as a part of the whole.

"Serious music, which sticks to the strict, life inhibiting rules of harmonics and the twelvetone system is not capable of creating a new culture."(Grandpierre: Marcus) Both classical and contemporary music "expect the audience's pregiven consent and forebearance. There are no participants here, just performers and listeners. Fake 'folk music', beyond its commercial uses is only good for damaging the word 'folk' and for frightening as many people as possible away from true 'folk music' Let's add to this the sleep inducing hits of light/ pop music and we can say that the overwhelming part of today's music is quite simply only good for exposing man to his own misery and for manipulating him so that he can be even more manipulated. The music that used to be so vigorous and alive that neither man nor animal could free himself from its magical power is now a disemboweled mammoth on tip-toes."(Grandpierre: Marcus)

"The chasm between musical experts and everyday musicians that has grown so wide in our culture makes people feel discouraged, and for some reason this is uniquely so with music. This performance chasm does seem to be cultural, specific to Western society." (Levitin, p. 194) In general, in the 20th century, the mainstream culture in the west has gone deeply into the capitalism of music and away from the concept of music for the people, by the people, thru this process of "glamorization" of music, the artists and the whole lifestyle around it. "The history of the American Music Industry is a disheartening one, which largely details the exploitation of artists and musicians by opportunists and those without the musician's best interests at heart." (Anonymous) Rock, pop and hip hop in particular have created an idolization of a lifestyle that is, for the most part, a relatively unhealthy one that is overly glamorized and filled with drugs, alcohol, sex, guns, and vanity. Just watch a few minutes of MTV or VH1, or look in a pop magazine and see what is being portrayed to our youth and the entire population as "cool," and you can easily get a concept of what is being "sold" en masse to mainstream society and in particular to our youth. I do recognize that there are artists who break this stereotype. I know several personally and greatly admire their (our) inner resolve to set a good example in an industry that sets a lot of poor examples of integrity, community and self respect. The reality is that those artists, overall, get a lot less media attention, and a lot less exposure to the people who really need to hear their messages and see their examples. Many of them are preaching to the choir really, performing for people who are already somewhat aware of their messages and in support of them. In the past few years, it seems there are more up and coming artists who are realizing the power they hold to influence their listeners and are making wonderful contributions to the world thru their arts. I look forward to the emergence of more of those beings. I also appreciate those elder artists who are setting positive examples by using their influence, money and success to launch humanitarian projects and serve the world, using the money machine of the music industry to serve some good and noble cause!

Disempowerment and The Decline of Music Making

"What is happening to raw music? Some people would rather listen to techno than create raw music. The very magic of synchronizing group music and dance is going away. A lot of tribal dance was dancing the same steps to create togetherness with the raw backbeat and magic that only drums, flutes, bells, stings, and singing can create. Dancing to a computer can never be the same to me."
                                        Johnny, Denver, CO

Where are the increasing numbers of people who can't get into the groove coming from? What has happened to them as children? What did not happen to or for them as children? "Why Janie Can't Groove" is certainly a book that needs to be written. I suspect that there are now two radically different ways to relate to music: 1) as a listener, associatively via the cortex, and 2) as a music making, participating, whole person. (Keil)

Making music together has shifted from a community sharing to a profession that has alienated the larger community from a very real and basic human experience. It has become a lost art form, something "scary" for non-musicians or "ordinary" people, and unfamiliar even to trained musicians in any out of context way. Many trained musicians can't improvise; they simply don't know how to play from the moment or their heart, it's been literally trained right out of them. In this shift, we have lost something very valuable. We've lost an inclusiveness, an openness and a willingness to play with each other, and in that, there has been a loss of intimacy and connection. The musical experience is more and more now dictated by the performer or DJ. The opportunity to experience true group expression thru chanting, music making and story telling is non-existant in the vast majority of bars, nightclubs or music venues. Music has become far more of a spectator sport and a commercial venture than a simple sharing of the human spirit. In my perspective, the commercialization of music is a major contributor to an overall feeling of dis-empowerment in ordinary, everyday people in relation to their own connection with music. For many adults, music was maybe in their lives as children, but for one reason or another they gave it up before they left highschool and never touched an instrument after that. Perhaps they quit because they didn't think they were "good enough," or "serious enough" or maybe because there is this illusion that everything we do as adults has to be for profit or "getting ahead." Playing music "just for fun" isn't enough of a good reason to do it when there are bills to pay and mouths to feed.

Music Making and Our Children

A study done in California reveals some interesting facts about the decline of music in our schools. "Participation in General Music courses (those courses designed to bring basic music knowledge and skills to young students) declined by 85.8% with the loss of 264,821 students. This represents over half of the total decline of participation in all Music Courses. This is followed by declines in other Music Courses (- 48.5%, -103,783 students), chorus (36.1%, -57,905 students), band (-20.5%, -44,509 students), and instrumental lessons (-41.4%, -39,792 students)." (Sound of Silence) This report was specific on California, but it holds a reflection of something that is happening not only in California, but nationwide, and in the western world. Canada and Europe have also applied huge cutbacks to their music and art programs thus greatly disabling generations of students from being exposed to music and art. In particular, however, music programs have taken the biggest hit in 2008 in our school systems.

Obviously, a music program costs a great deal of money for equipment, instruments, extra faculty and space in the school, and when the governing bodies of western culture are looking at ways to continue to pay for wars, weapons and the upcoming oil crisis, amongst other corporate interests, music and the arts are quickly targeted as "unnecessary" extracurricular activities. While cuts in music programs create the illusion of saving money, the students previously in music groups are then shifted to smaller classes which then require more teachers and thus more money to fund. While a band director may often typically have 100 students and sometimes more in a class period, other teachers generally have fewer. In my high school, there were over 100 students in my band "class." It was the only class I ever had that was over 30 students. If instrumental music classes are cut, even more teachers will be needed to supervise those same 100 students in other classes. The ultimate cost of cutting music programs is more than that of maintaining the programs. (John Benham: Garcia)

As discussed earlier, western culture simply doesn't have the same kind of relationship with music as more traditional cultures do. Music is more for the purpose of entertainment than a lifestyle, more of a spectator sport than a participatory community activity of sharing and learning together. It is more of a commercialized "game" than a valuable social institution. Music isn't woven into our daily existence in the same way at all, and so it isn't always considered a necessary component to a child's development or survival by policy makers and those who control the flow of resources to the schools. In addition, there's no standardized test that has a music section, so it gets cut before a lot of other things. (Writer) Meanwhile, it has been proven time and time again, that music students are more well-rounded and do better on tests than other students and that music gives them a skill they can take with them for the rest of their lives.

In addition, surveys have shown repeatedly that the decline in music participation in our schools conflicts with public opinion. A nationwide 2003 Gallup poll found that 93 percent of Americans feel schools should offer musical instruction as part of the regular curriculum, and a California Public Opinion Survey released in 2001 by the California Arts Council found that 89 percent of Californians believe the arts help children develop creative skills, and 74 percent of them believe the arts improve the quality of children's overall education. (Sound of Silence)

"The 1997 American Attitudes Towards Music poll found an overwhelming 93 percent of the respondents agreed that music is part of a well-rounded education, and 86 percent felt all schools should offer instrumental music as part of the regular curriculum; 71 percent said states should mandate music education for every child. Community financial support for school music education was endorsed by 85 percent of those asked. And 97 percent believe music helps channel children's energy in a creative way. Other benefits of school music cited by the respondents of this survey include:

  *Developing teamwork skills (96 percent)

  *Helping children to get along with others (84 percent)

  *Better grades and test scores (70 percent).

  *Music helps a child's overall intellectual development (88%)

"Of the respondents who play an instrument, 85 percent began between the ages of five and fourteen...and 96 percent said learning to play is something they will always be glad they did." (Garcia/A Big Yes for Music)

The decline of music making in the schools and in our youth is a major contributing factor to the decline of music making in the western cultures in general. Again, seeing our children as holding the blueprint for the future, there is much to consider. Finding ways to make music making fun, exciting and approachable by all ages of children and helping to empower them to play, dance and sing will make a better world for all of us in the future.

Charles Keil, of MUSE, Inc is a sociomusicologist, teacher and musician who works with children in the schools in NY teaching drum, dance and what he calls "musiking" (Music Making).

"For over 25 years I have been offering classes in Afro-Latin drumming at the university. Every semester I have to turn away highly motivated students who love music, listen to it constantly, but can't master the most basic coordinations after practicing hours and hours for a week. Two different clave rhythms clapped with the hands against a steady 4/4 tap of the foot is all that I require as an audition. If 15% of the motivated and eager students can't do it, what percentage of the students overall are unable to keep together in dance or song, hold a tune, sing and drum at the same time? I suspect that a growing majority of Americans can't musick or dance in time, and that it is mostly young people pacified by TV and deskbound schooling that are swelling the ranks of the 'musically unexpressed.'" (Keil)

Keil goes on to say, that our culture has been musically "systematically incapacitated:" all ages, all races, all socioeconomic groups. (Keil 1990) Keil talks about several "incapacities" that he has named to be the Inability to entrain or work with others, self consciousness, lack of coordination, and visual dependency. In examining these, the familiar story emerges again. All of these "incapacities" that Keil talks about are easily recognizable by-products of our culture: insufficient socialization leads to lack of coordination and the inability to work with others, extreme independence can contribute to the same, being sat in front of the TV or computer screen creates a visual dependency, and lack of recognition or proper socialization can easily create a self conscious being who isn't sure if they're doing the right thing or not, and is afraid of being seen either way.

The concept that most caught my attention, in Keil's work, however was that of the Hyper-cultured youth. The effects of electronic music, which has become a dominating force in today's popular and commercial music are showing up in interesting ways in the youth of today. Here is what he shares on this from his 25 years of experience in the field: "Young people who have listened to a lot of loud rock, reverbed, delayed, echoed, overdubbed, electronic, overproduced, multi-tracked, etc., etc. music, develop a different kind of hearing, an esthetics, a definition of music, that may not let them grasp the subtleties of timing when it comes to making music with others. The drug experiences that often go with loud techno-expanded rock may also be a factor when something is seeming wrong with the fine tuning, the micro-timing of a person's participation." (Keil)

A great percentage of the young population today is so caught up in the techno/computer world of the internet, games and technology that making music just isn't even a consideration in their world. Music is now just what they might be listening to on I-tunes or Napster as the hottest new hit for ninety nine cents, or what they're going to "go and see" next. There are innumerable factors to consider, as always. The busy life, the lack of time, the lack of spaces or opportunities to explore, the glamorization of music implying you have to look hot and be sexy, and the increasing technological demands around the music realm all contribute in their own ways to a decline of people playing instruments, singing and dancing together.

Many young people just don't believe they can do it. They see the stars on TV, and because for the most part, in modern culture, that's what's offered and visible as what it means to be a "musician," they don't realize the vast possibilities outside the Music "Industry" that exist or can be created. Add to that the western concept mentioned earlier, in chapter 3, that the western mind views music as some "special" gift and it is easy to see how insecurities can develop and then be fully supported by the modern culture we are emesshed in!

As a rhythm and drumming teacher and facilitator, I encounter regularly people who firmly believe that they aren't musical or rhythmical, "can't" do that, "don't have any rhythm," and on and on. However, what I invariably find, is that the people who believe the story of "I can't," or "I don't have rhythm" the most, almost always have perfect timing and an untapped resevoir of potential within them that they were talked out of, often at an early age. When they begin to discover their own abilities, it opens up worlds of new possibilities for them and it's almost as if their lives begin anew.

If we give our children the opportunity to create a solid foundation in music, they will grow up knowing that it is part of life, and not just for the "stars." By re-empowering the youth, we re-empower generations of music making, well rounded individuals! And if we, as adults, give ourselves permission to play and express ourselves creatively thru the muses, we set an example for our children that sets the foundation for the re-emergence of heart sharings, community music making and more harmony in our world! Music is well known to be a universal language and it's applications are vast for peace keeping, conflict resolution and global communication! Sharing it and keeping it alive in the youth offers unlimited potentiality for the future of our world!

Chapter 5

Nightclubs, Bars
and
Community Dances

"Bars are not for listening. You don't go to a bar to hear a band. You go to see friends, consume intoxicants, and SEE a band. Not that there's anything inherently wrong with that. But most musicians don't want to be seen. They want to be heard. As a musician, I speak from experience. And it's hard to compete with conversational noise in a bar (not to mention all the other noises). Another factor: alcohol is the wrong drug for listening. Alcohol and cocaine are "talking drugs.""

Neville Harson, Boulder, CO

"It is easy to see that the whole foundation of bars, nightclubs and the techno tribal "trance" experiences that modern day culture is expressing is really an ancient community experience. It is a capatalistic attempt to re-create an experience, a feeling, a space and possibly community that is very much part of human history, and a practical rarity in today's world. It is creating an entire culture of half deaf alcoholics who really in their heart of hearts are seeking avenues for human connection, community sharings, and higher states of consciousness and who deeply share a love of music, trance and dance."

Cheri Shanti, from article "Re-connecting our Roots"

The music is thumping. The bass goes right thru me and my body is effortlessly coerced into movement. My feet move in rhythm to the music. It is easy to delve into trance and forget everything in the music. In an instant I am fully present to the moment. All the drama of my life is invisible, melting away thru the bass. I close my eyes, and an inner world opens up instantly. Colors come thru from the music's vibrations. Forms pulse with the beats into kaleidoscopic visions of light inside my self. A tunnel of swirling colors opens and I enter it. My body and my consciousness are unified yet I am no longer my body. I am larger than life, towering above the physical realms like a giant. I am this freedom. I am this grace. I am unified with a greater aspect of my being. I feel the bliss of being and I am free! Then I feel an elbow jab me in the jaw, and my eyes open to the sensation of pain. Next to me swirling wildly, a young man with a glass of beer is reeling in his own inner realms, beer spilling all over me, him and the floor. His eyes are openly violating my personal space with his lustful vibe. I move away from him to another corner of the dance floor. Looking around, and forgetting him, I am entranced by the energy once again, but now I am studying, observing, seeing the world I'm in and feeling a little less safe, a lot more protective and not nearly as soft inside.

Almost everyone is dancing, many of them holding beers and swirling wildly also, looking as if they might fall over any moment, but I'm looking at something beyond that. I'm seeing an energy field that is being created in this place. I'm seeing the release of life tensions and stress, I'm seeing the human spirit and it's need for expression in the dancers, and I'm seeing the deeper call for connection that every one there, conscious of it or not, is feeling. Sadly, I'm also seeing the symptoms of a sick culture in the rampant abuse of drugs and alcohol, with easily seventy five percent or more of the people there either high, drinking or already drunk and stumbling visibly. For a moment I wonder how many of them have a close place to fall down in and how many will have to drive to their lonely homes again at 2 am when the club closes. I am deeply touched by their sadness and can see in their vacant eyes how lost they feel, how confused and how overwhelmed they are. To be honest, I can even relate to it, I know the feeling too, I have experienced it plenty! I am mostly amazed by the tenacity of the human spirit: here at 1 am, most having worked 8-10 hours today and going back to it early in the morning. Yet we/they are here, night after night dancing, drinking and trying to feel something in this world that matters more than their day jobs, or that makes them feel more alive.

I spent a lot of time in clubs in my teens and twenties. It was a huge part of my life because I needed to dance and I needed connection with others in that space. I needed a place where I could shut my mouth and quiet my brain and just *feel life* within me. I needed it like water. When I was young, I would often break down and cry in my room at night because I had this unyielding dream, a call of sorts, to dance with people around a fire, and pray thru my body. Raised in an ultra-conservative home and environment, I had no idea what this was about at that early age, only that somewhere in my bones, I felt like I had been stuffed into the wrong body, in the wrong time and I was misplaced. I had my own bedroom ritual where I'd put on headphones and dance for hours until I was sweating like crazy, or until I collapsed on the ground. My parents always thought I was doing homework! I was such a good student they just assumed all that time was in the books. I couldn't tell them, they just wouldn't understand, they still don't! I was raised in a family that had very little appreciation for the arts. Life was about work (and work isn't supposed to be fun or joyful), and making as much money as possible. All else is a frivolous waste of time, except nature I suppose. My father really instilled a deep love of nature in me.

I am most grateful for that! And truly Nature is the highest form of Art created by the Artists of all Artists for us to enjoy and explore!

Dancing was an irreplaceable part of my medicine, and I had to have my fix. It was my release, my freedom, my way out of the social confinements that I felt in my family and my culture, and it was a place I felt like I could relate to people who had some understanding of what mattered in life. There's no way to explain it, but somehow in my early pre-teens and teens, I just knew that people who could get free in their bodies, people who could and would move were more alive, more passionate, more willing to experience life rather than just watch it go by. I wanted to be one of those people: alive, passionate and excited by life. I guess I was a bit of a groove addict, even then, maybe more so then as there was definitely more of a need. I started going to dance clubs very young. There was the roller rink, where I'd go for all day skate on Sunday's. It was all about the music and dancing on my skates: the slow dances, the races, the groovy 70's disco music and mostly connecting with people my age who understood what I was going thru.

In my early teens, there was a youth dance club that I was allowed to go to, and my girlfriends and I would dance it up and get wild there on the weekend nights. When I went home for my 20 year class reunion I was deeply touched by several high school friends reminiscing on dancing with me "back in the day." "Cheri you got me to dance. Rememer the Library, that teen club, and you'd get out there when no one else was dancing and get the whole place rocking." Another one said, "If it wasn't for you Cheri, maybe I would never have danced." One of these women is now a professional competing dancer in Salsa, the other is also a performing artist. I had no idea what I was inspiring, I just wanted to share the dance floor with my friends and boogy down! By the time I was 15 I was getting into the "adult" bars and clubbing it heavy in Hollywood and Miami, and because I looked and acted older than 15, I was never questioned, and never asked for ID. At that time it was still 18 and over so it was easy work to give the doorman a wink and a smile and scoot in to get my groove on.

In college, I was still a full blown dance junky. I was exploring participating in the culture around the clubs, the drinking and even some dabbling in psychedelics, and ecstasy. I share this because in writing this chapter I am not coming from an outsider's perspective in any way! I can easily say that some of my first trance experiences happened in these clubs and it was definitely a significant part of my life for learning my body, my dance, and my own unique relationship to rhythm. When I was dancing, I wanted no interruptions. I had no tolerance for men hitting on me, or people trying to talk to me; though I did warmly invited those who I could tell were kindred spirits in the dance whom I knew I could just play with without any disruption to my space. I wanted to be completely in the music, to become the music, to experience every syncopation, every sound, every vibration that it had to offer me. I'm still very much like this when I go out to hear music. I'm there to be submerged, too experience the fullness of the artists, and to go deeper into myself. I learned a really valuable musical skill thru that experience: an ability to feel music right to the core of my being. I found myself knowing the changes in the music before they came, even in songs I'd never heard before. I learned music thru my body and could anticipate shifts and changes with finess and total accuracy. I discovered that I had a natural capacity to feel subtle nuances of music that weren't actually IN the music, but that came thru the mergings of different frequencies and that my body could assimilate them thru movement. I found myself hearing melodies and parts *thru my body* that weren't in the music itself and this was the beginning of creating songs thru rhythm.

Beyond the powerful deep personal experiences and openings, I had a tribe and learned invaluable social skills thru these experiences. I knew when I went to the clubs that I could find people who felt my joy and my pain, people who would witness my dance and see the truths it held. I would often have people comment on my dancing. I was noticed there by others who had an appreciation for free expression and movement. I could learn by watching others dance how to read someone's energy. I learned how to see where people held pain by the way they moved, and was able to gain wisdom just by observing someone dance. I learned how to create strong, yet flexible boundaries that protected me while still allowing for the human exchange of energy. I saw and skirted sketchy situations where someone did or could have gotten really hurt thru the wisdom gained by watching energy, and knowing when things were cool and safe, and when they weren't. I was able to apply these skills even on the streets and in school, and found myself able to move through life with more fluidity, more flexibility and more willingness to surrender than many of my young friends and I was often sought out for counsel by my peers. I can honestly say that I feel it was all from the music and the dance, and it was the music and the dancing that made me stand out amongst others my age. I was learning myself deeper, knowing myself in a way that was inspiring, and empowering to those around me as well as myself.

Luckily, while my love affair with dance and community has never waned, my curiosity for altered states induced by alcohol or substances exited fairly rapidly! The truth is, I learned pretty quickly that it wasn't the alcohol or "x" that got me to the altered state I was seeking. It was the music and my body's responsiveness to it. I learned that I could get much higher and escape the crashes if I just went out to the same clubs, and danced all night without any substances or artifical highs! I had gotten there for years before the substances ever came in, so I knew it was *me* and not the substance that was the portal to higher states. I had always been a spiritual being, even as a very young child, so I knew "God" or "Spirit" held infinite energy for me. I also knew that I wanted my life to be an example of what is possible naturally. I am a firm believer that you can't know anything unless you've experienced it, and for me experiencing both possibilities gave me the wisdom and true perspective I personally needed to speak with authenticity about the natural state of beingness!

Now, looking at the Night club scene, I can see it from a very real and personal perspective. I fully understand the deeper needs that draw us into these environments: the need to belong, to have community, to celebrate, release, dance, be witnessed, to learn by witnessing others, to learn social skills, and to practice them, to learn our own boundaries and how to be clear with them, to surrender to music, trance and our deeper selves in a safe and designated place for altered states of consciousness. And for some of us, to touch God and be in communion with spirit through our bodies and share that with others having a similar experience. "People in a groove experience a kind of altered state of consciousness, perhaps a light trance. Socially, people grooving together are unified." (Farmelo) The club culture somehow gives us a community connection, a human connection, and something that feels like an ancient primal pulse: tribal and tangible.

I often look at bars and clubs as an attempt to re-create the Tribal aspects of music that western culture is missing. I guess it was several years ago that this first came to me. I think of what it may have been like in a village somewhere when people got restless and needed to have a release of energies. They needed to dance and sing and be together in ways that weren't about just everyday life, but in ways that touched the mystical aspect of humanness, and the spirit world. Each culture had it's medicine, and it's way of calling forth the tribe, the neighboring villages, sometimes even their enemies, for a night of dancing and celebrating life. I imagine that the music was loud and went late into the night. People were dancing, trancing, singing and taking medicines, or maybe spirits (alcohol), maybe mushrooms, maybe smoking plants that created altered states. Each individual there in their own way of connecting with Spirit, some as dancers, some drumming, some singing, some making food, some serving, some visioning, etc. but large groups of people all together with the same music, the same vibrations coursing thru their bodies creating a shared experience.

So in looking at what the mainstream western culture has created to give some kind of space for the tribal experience, the closest thing I can relate it to is a bar or nightclub where there is regularly music, dancing and often a lot of intoxication. "For many of its devotees, this club culture represents an escape from the regimentation of modern life and even a return to a pre-industrial pagan shamanistic utopia. United on the dance floor, revellers of different ethnic backgrounds, sexual orientations and ages dance wall-to-wall, sweating, smiling and enjoying the DJ's clever acoustic tricks. The combination of loud, rhythmic music and visual distortion heightens the collective spirit as the sound enters the crowd—machine rhythms, pounding drums, overlaid with a gospel spirituality of peace, love and unity." (Hillegonda)

Bars and clubs are in the perfect place to capitalize on the vital human need of being together in these ways, and in today's world they are also capitalizing on people's disconnection, depression and anxiety just as much. Many people go to these establishments looking to connect, searching for someone or something outside of themselves that may bring them a night or a moment of connection. Bars create a community of sorts, but when people get in their cars and drive away, they are just as alone and disconnected as before they went. In tribal gatherings it is truly an experience of acknowledging a shared existence, they are already connected and live, breathe, eat and exist together in closer proximity. This for me is an interesting distinction between traditional cultures and the modern western culture I live in. Bars serve a purpose in this way to allow space for this kind of connection.

Another thing that is worthy of noting is that the tribal experience has no "star," there is no glamorization of the music or those playing it. Certainly outstanding masterful players or dancers are recognized and appreciated, but it isn't something put up on a pedastal the way we put our performers up on a stage, charge money to see them, and glamorize their very existance, watching them constantly to see what they do in private, who they're smooching and where they eat cheeseburgers. The whole scene in modern America supports the Glamorization of music and the idolization of the "artists." The Industry behind it really works hand in hand at keeping the separation between audience and performer pretty distinct and recognizable. As a performer in modern culture, I can also understand the need for that, so there's no judgement, just an observation on the distinction.

In today's world, my premise is we need a balance; we need both. I certainly am not advocating that we give one up for the other, on the contrary. I would just like to open up possibilities for more balance, and to invite people back into the process of participation in the music! There needs to be a certain understood space between performers and audience when the show is "on" and I understand the need for protecting that space! A consideration, however, is a simple willingness to meet and acknowledge each other: performer to observor, in neutral space, perhaps after or before the performances. This creates an inclusiveness and a certain basic human bond that builds continuity and community. One band that always impressed me with their abilty to acknowledge and share with their fans is the Flecktones. After their shows, they always come out and spend time talking one on one with fans. They share experiences, hear from their fans, and also offer insights to them. It's truly a beautiful thing. They are humble and sincere in their appreciation for their fans and they show it in this way when they commune and acknowledge their humanness and love of music together with their fans!

Community Dance Creations:
Offering Alternatives to Nightclubs

"In order for live music to evolve, the audience has to change. And in order for the audience to change, the context and rules (written and unwritten) of the space has to change."

Neville Harson

I am blessed to live in Boulder, CO where there is a relatively large and active community of people in the sub-culture now commonly referred to as the "Cultural Creatives." Cultural Creatives is a term that was coined by world-renowned sociologist Paul H. Ray and psychologist Sherry Ruth Anderson to describe an emerging sub-set of the world population that has recently developed beyond the standard paradigm of Modernists versus Traditionalists or Conservatists, which we can also look at as Democrats or Republicans. They found that 50 million adult Americans (slightly over one quarter of the adult population) can now be identified as belonging to this group. This growing section of the population is admittedly spiritual and embraces the practice of spiritual values in daily life without formal religion (Anderson and Ray, 2000). Cultural creatives tend to become familiar with a variety of religions and seek to identify with principles that are universal amongst religions, finding the truths more important than the dogma. Cultural Creatives have an appreciation for nature, the arts, community and family. They uphold strong virtues around integrity, transparency and teamwork. In 2007 I had a chance to see Paul Ray in person and participate in a community workshop he was doing in Boulder. I was deeply inspired to learn that this sub-culture, the Cultural Creatives, is now approximately 30% of the population *globally.* This to me is inspiring and exciting news for the future of our planet on most every level imaginable.

When I consider it in context to the topic at hand, and in conjunction with the sharings of many people in different environments I visit, it is clear that there is a growing demand for alternatives to bars and nightclubs where alcohol and mainstream music are all that are offered. There is a whole group of people now who are hungry for something that creates bonds, and offers an opportunity to feel a part of something. They are looking for music that has a deeper message than heartbreak, or lust, and for music that invites a community of people who want to go deeper than just the typical bar scene, small talk and meaningless connections.

The Rave Culture that emerged full force in the 90's was of significance in recent history of providing an alternative to bars that met many of these social needs while holding also a different intention than what the mainstream culture was offering thru nightclubs. In addition, it gave a space for many of the Cultural Creatives of today to explore, express and be together. The word rave (and various derivatives) was first used to describe Bohemian Parties happening in the UK in the 1950-60s and actually originated from people of Caribbean descent living in London at that time. In the late 1980s, the word "rave" was adopted to describe the subculture that grew out of the acid house movement. (Wikkapedia) The history of the Rave scene is a fascinating one that somewhat holds parallels to the youth movements of the 60's in that there is a strong interest in non-violence and music. In addition the culture holds values for peace, love, respect, unity and personal responsibility. It is many of those early ravers who are now rising to the occasion of creating healthier dance alternatives to the world in their communities. The Rave Culture generated a counter-culture movement that is still alive today, and definitely got the attention of government officials for it's ability to draw large crowds of people together. In the U.S., the mainstream media and law enforcement agencies have branded the subculture as a purely drug-centric culture similar to the hippies of the 1960s. As a result, ravers have been effectively run out of business in many areas.

In my home community of Boulder, CO, groups have popped up all over creating their own dance clubs of sorts. Groups like Boulder Dance Home, Gypsie Nation, Family Moons Productions and others are creating viable alternatives to the night club dance scenes that provide all of the same social needs that clubs do, and more. People are throwing more "trance" parties in private homes or renting out local centers, decorating and creating their own night clubs for a night a week, or a month. These gatherings have shown to be very successful and there is a strong network of people who keep them going and growing. This is happening all over the country!

From what I've experienced, there is a strong awareness in these alternative communities that humans need each other, and that everyone who comes makes a difference and is participating in creating the experience. Those who frequent them share a willingness to connect with each other and to be seen. There is a deep desire to heal on an individual and global level. It's not unusual at these kinds of events to see people trading massages, doing healing work, or engaged in deep and meaningful conversation. The sexual energy and lustful vibes that are so prevalent in bars, is there of course, but to a lesser extent because many of the people are there for something deeper and more long lasting than a one nighter and often they are alcohol free which will certainly change the vibration of any party. There is a concern for cultivating relationship and maintaining respect between each other.

Of course, there are always deviations, but in general, there is a higher consciousness permeating the room. Often there is an opening and closing circle where all present will come together to pray or hold an intention or share. This in and of itself creates a much different awareness. Imagine going to a bar and looking at each person in a circle and recognizing the humanness in them and the reflection it holds for you in your life. It simply changes our interactions, inviting a more human, respectful and sacred possibility of seeing each other.

These groups are all a step in the right direction to support the Cultural Creatives, and the growing population of beings who are actively seeking deeper connections, more community and support in their lives. I believe they are all significant parts of a greater whole and worthy of recognition in this journey towards transformation.

Considering all of this, I see vast potential for the night club scene to take an evolutionary step forward to assist in transforming our world thru musical sharings more in line with these intentions. There are so many ways that these already existing establishments could serve a greater good than people getting intoxicated. There is a shift happening, and it is moving us towards a higher consciousness, healthier beings, healthier communities and more awareness of our interconnectivity.

Considerations of Over Amplified Music and Electronic Music

"A study in Britain found that of those who went to rock concerts up to 73 per cent reported dulled hearing or tinnitus or both. Among clubbers the figure was 66 per cent, and 17 per cent of stereo users also reported hearing difficulties. Tests have shown that 44 per cent of those who attend rock concerts once a month have hearing difficulties." (Murray)

"In the absence of loud noises, hearing doesn't appear to deteriorate much with age." (FDA)

One of the main reasons I've gotten turned off to going out to see bands or DJ's at bars or clubs, is that the music is so loud that it literally hurts me. I can feel it, not only my ears and head, but inside my body. I'm sensitive yes, but mainly because I have chosen to not deafen myself, so I can actually still hear and feel. I have been very conscious in recent years of wearing ear plugs, and leaving if the sound is too much for me. It is also one of the reasons I stopped gigging at bars as I could tell that I was being affected and my ears and head hurt after a night of loud music. That ringing sound took some time to fade back into the sound of stillness. I have a theory that I joke about, but I am also 100% serious, that a lot of soundmen are at least partially deaf from the years of listening to music way over the volume threshold that is healthy. Because they are partially deaf, they continue to pump up the volume and the bass even when is already deafening because they have blown out their natural capacity to hear the same highs and lows that a healthy normal ear can hear. A good percentage of the clubbers are partially deaf as well, so few notoice, and even fewer will have the courage to speak up when it's painful.

Many musicians begin to lose their hearing over time from the super high sound levels that get cranked thru speakers, monitors and their day to day worlds as performers. A consistent concert goer is certain to have some damage after a certain amount of shows, it's just inevitable. The statistics show that more and more young people are suffering hearing loss, and at increasingly younger ages. "Many young people are at risk of premature hearing loss," according to the Royal National Institute for Deaf People. They blame the growth in the popularity of loud music for what they says is an "alarming rise in deafness among the young."

Consider this: the human eardum hears frequencies between 20Hz to 20,000 Hz. Decibels (dB) are the measurement of sound "pressure," and humans can hear sounds as low as -15 dB. Damage to the human auditory system occurs at sounds above 85 dB. With extended exposure, noises that reach a decibel level of 85 can cause permanent damage to the hair cells in the inner ear, leading to hearing loss. To gain context on what this means, consider the following: a typical conversation occurs at 50-60 dB, this is not loud enough to cause any damage. A bulldozer that is idling (note that this is idling, not actively bulldozing) is loud enough at 85 dB that it can cause permanent damage after only 1 work day. When listening to music on earphones at a standard volume level 5, the sound generated reaches a level of 100 dB which is loud enough to cause permanent damage after just 15 minutes a day. According to the NIOSH (The National Insitute for Occuupational Safety and Health) and the CDC (Center for Disease Prevention and Control), at 85 dB the permissible exposure before permanent damage occurs to our ears is 8 hours. At 115 dB, it is .46875 min or approximately 30 seconds. To give more perspective: 120 decibels is 1,000 per cent louder than 85 decibels, and 150 dB is twice as loud as a jet taking off or the crack of a gunshot.

Concerts and clubs amplify music at a range of 95-150 dB. The now popular "all-nighters" means that dancers are exposed to these high levels for long periods of time, which means, inevitably, damage to the auditory systems of those present. Even with ear plugs at the highest rating in the stores, 33 decibles, it's not going to fully prevent damage at these levels. Another interesting consideration is that workers are required by law to be offered ear protection if they are subject to noise above 85 decibels, yet there are no statutory limits for the protection of audiences at concerts, clubs or dance parties. Even a one time experience can produce lasting damage, so for those who are going out nightly, or weekly and being exposed to this kind of sound there is a very high likeliehood of permanent hearing loss. Hearing loss and impairment has become very common in young people and is no longer related to age at all. The past 20 years has shown a huge increase in the incidence of Noise Induced Hearing Loss in our youth. I find it criminal that it is allowed, but that's just me! I find it even more amazing how unaware most people are to what they are exposing themselves to, and the lack of concern when they are made aware, it's typically just a shrug and an "Oh well."

Sound is a very powerful energy and the effects of it on the human system are well documented and no big mystery any more. Above the audible range for humans is ultrasound and below it is infrasound. Although largely unheard, sound in these ranges affects the human body in ways that are quite profound. In addition to the levels of sound at clubs and dance parties, the frequencies that are being emitted from the speakers and their effects to the human system are worthy of noting. The bass that gets pumped through at those 95 dB and over levels is significant and can be felt all the way thru the body. Unprotected exposure to bass (infrasound) frequencies at those decibels can also create a loss of balance along with the damage to the ear itself. Perhaps why those intoxicated at clubs seem to reel and fall all over themselves more than usual!

In the 1960's, NASA scientists produced most of the documentation of the effects of infrasound on the human body. They were particularly keen to discover how proximity to the low frequencies produced by rocket engines would affect their astronauts, especially during launching. Their extensive tests confirmed that, at certain volumes, infrasound did indeed have various physiological consequences. According to results published by NASA researcher GH Mohr, frequencies between 0Hz and 100Hz, at up to 150-155dB, produced vibrations of the chest wall, changes in respiratory rhythm, gagging sensations, headaches, coughing, visual distortion, and post-exposure fatigue. Subsequent research has determined that the frequency that causes vibration of the eyeballs – and therefore distortion of vision – is around 19Hz. It has also been speculated that exposure to certain infrasound frequencies could stimulate aggression and exacerbate psychological disturbances. (Seargant) To relate this to concerts and clubs: there are speakers on the market now available and in use for clubs that are rated as low as 18Hz and cranking music out of them at levels up to 150 dB for extended periods of time, often all night long. If you seriously consider the physiology of the human body in this context, it would seem difficult to not consider how these frequencies are affecting people in bars and at concerts: the violence that often happens, the uneasiness in the body, the tiredness the next day after a show, etc. The hangover may not be just from the alcohol after all! The body doesn't lie!

The impacts of excessively long and loud music to the human system can be similar to a low grade "Sonic Weapon." Sonic weapons have been used throughout history and are being worked on now to control, numb, quiet and disorient the enemy. Both ultrasound and infrasound frequencies can damage, and even kill humans. "According to the Working Paper on Infrasound Weapons produced by Hungary for the United Nations in 1978, the frequency that is thought to be most dangerous to humans is between 7 and 8Hz. This is the resonant frequency of flesh and, theoretically, it can rupture internal organs if loud enough. Seven hertz is also the average frequency of the brain's alpha rhythms; thus this frequency has been described as dangerous but also relaxing." (Seargant) Basically, this is what happens, of course on a different level, at a concert or a club when the human body is exposed to unnaturally loud sound with super low bass and sub-bass frequencies for hours at a time. The super low frequencies that you can't hear in the bass are the most dangerous ones. Although some part of it feels good, if you can feel that going all the way thru your body, there is more to consider than just the feel good aspects, and possibly the rest of your life to be affected by your choices!

"Therapeutically, music can be a tremendous intervention. It can relieve pain and stress, calm the heart rate and blood pressure, affect physical responses for healing and growth, and stimulate creative thinking, he said. (Arthur Harvey, U of HI Professor) But some music should be avoided. Excessively dissonant, loud and repetitive music such as electronica or techno can affect thinking, behavior and hearing. "And if you're impacted by emotional pulses, you tend to behave in a way that's not always rational." (Altonn)

Electronic music is an interesting topic for me. I like some of it, a lot of it, especially beautifully done music with elements of world beat, beautiful vocals, and funky conscious hip hop. As I already mentioned, I've had some really powerful experiences dancing to electronic beats and techno grooves. Several years ago, I had an insight that really made me question the levels to which this music can affect us. I was watching a young man dance. His moves were so machine like, completely unnatural, and still somehow very cool of course. In my musically altered and open state of consciousness, I saw deeper than just the dance and the dancer, and I saw this young being taking on machine like consciousness. That may sound strange to many people, but it's what I saw and I have witnessed it many times since then in many different dance environments. It's something happening internally that I'm seeing in these young people that I'm not sure fully how to express. All I can say is that I see a human body taking on machine like energy and motion, and again, I hold no judgement, this is just an observation.

In addition, and on a purely esthetic level, electronic music lacks the groove, the nuances and subtleties that only live music can create. It can hold the emotive energies of the producer, or DJ, but it simply isn't able to respond fully like a live human to the energy of a space, situation or experience. "Musicians generally agree that groove works best when it is not metronomic, that is when it's not perfectly machinelike. The gold standard of groove is usually a drummer who changes the tempo slightly according to aesthetic and emotional nuances of the music; we say then that the rhythm track, that the drums, "breathe." (Levitin)

The computer generated music that has inundated the music industry is not going to go away, and I would never propose that it does! It induces trance and works on the human system in it's own unique ways, and it has created a whole culture within itself. Any coming together of people to share in the groove is worthy of recognition, and a lot of the electronic music scene is based on love, community and respect with unparallaled creative freedom for dress, dance and more! The possibilities for creativity with electronic music have only begun to be experienced and I expect we will see more and more interactive musical experiences thru it in the coming years. The electronic movement has brought forth whole new sounds, vibrations and opened new portals to human creativity that were simply not possible before!

Of course, my vision is to merge the ancient and the future, bring the roots of community participatory music making into the picture, blend it in and see what emerges! I expect we will see amazing new opportunities in this realm as people continue to seek ways to connect human to human thru musical interactions! The magic, the mystery, the Muse!

Chapter 6

Community Music Making

"In the United States alone, millions of people buy millions of records and spend millions of dollars on concert tickets. MTV is one of the largest successes of the century. Yet, active, physical, human participation in the processes of live music and dance affirms life in ways that can not be bought or sold."(Farmelo)

"The benefits of Recreational Music Making extend far beyond music. It ultimately affords unparalleled creative expression that unites our bodies, minds and spirits."
Karl T Bruhn

"The experience of music making is much richer and more complex than conventional western esthetics allows, since in experiencing the relationships in music making we are experiencing the relationships of the wider world as we conceive them to be and as we believe they ought to be." (Small)

Before bars, nightclubs, and techno there was the art of Making Music together as a community. Drummers, with hands on skin, played all night long with dancers sweating, singing, chanting and grooving for ceremonies, celebrations and even the "normal" days in between. People gathered where the music was, and celebrated the human experience together humbly as a participatory experience where everyone was part of the magic. Each person's contribution was part of creating something greater for everyone and everyone was invited to be active in the dance, in the music, and in the experience. It wasn't just the young 20 somethings that came out like in a lot of the "scenes" of the modern world. The whole community was drawn together: grandmas, the kids, brothers, sisters, friends, the whole tribe came together to be a part of something that broke the mundane and gave allowance for something deeper and more meaningful to come thru. Some may call it "entertainment" now, but the roots of music culture is community based and much more of a Participatory Experience than a Spectator Sport. It was people singing together, sharing stories and life experiences thru the dance, thru the songs, thru stories, and they were witnessing each other in life.

Keepin it Live!

A live music experience is a two-way sharing process: those playing the music share it with those listening, dancing or observing; and they in turn share their energy with those playing the music. This melding is not just communication, or the processing of information, but communion." (Meyers 1967:Ch1) (Farmelo)

"Another amazing night of music, drumming, dancing, sweating the stress out of the bones of my being! This medicine of community music is, for me, far more than anything else can give me. It's real, it's tangible, it's hands moving, eyes seeing, feet pounding, body shaking, soul resurrecting truth beyond anything else.

"And the amazingness of *real* people, not hpyed up on a stage, not separated by the over amplification of electronics, but sharing the floor together, all at the same level of being. Witnessing, and being witnessed. Singing and *being* the song, dancing and *being* the dance, Praying and *being* the prayer creating something magical together. The sweetness of being, such a deep and profound truth of human experience that we, with our modern culture, dj's and over amplified sounds have forgotten as a people.

"I give thanks to those who are keeping this way of being alive. Those who still play music together for the love of community and sharing, for the experience of depth that it offers and the undeniable bond that it forms between us as humans on this swirling planet earth. Untrained, real, raw voices are more beautiful than any trained one to my ears."
Journal Entry: Cheri Shanti, Oct, 2007

As someone who has participated heavily in both the tribal drum and dance worlds and the trance dance, DJ/Nightclub communities on all levels, from going just to dance, or just to play, to promoting and sponsoring events, to playing music for them, holding space quietly, watching and observing, and cleaning up the crap left over, I have a fairly wide range of experiences! I see the value in all of it, and in my life, I see that this path has been an evolution of my soul. Each piece has contributed an irreplaceable piece to who I am, what I know to be truth, and how I choose to dance thru life: as an observer or a participant in each unique opportunity.

For me, the journey has led me to feel fully, without any questioning, that there is simply no replacement for live, in the moment, participatory music making. Nothing else holds the mystery, the magic or the passionate spark of total creativity that it does. Nothing else can bring me to the depths and heights of my humanness in the same way. It provides me context to have compassion, to want to share, to be seen, to be witnessed and held by others, and to offer all of that back in service to something beyond myself. It teaches me how to communicate, how to listen with my heart, how to get out of my own way, and how to balance my individuality in a group context. And the spontaneity and ability for truly in the moment experiences always keeps me coming back for more as I am always touched by what emerges.

In my personal experience, many of the "trance" dances or Ecstatic dances and DJ parties (where electronica music is used) get stuck in the stagnancy of repetition and are missing a vital piece. Often the music is either a DJ or a CD which can only go so far to respond to the energy that is present in the moment. When music is chosen before an experience actually happens, or a DJ has only a certain repetoire to choose from, it does not allow for the full expression of spontaneity, nor does it allow for the group consciousness to surface authentically. It instead leads and often dictates where the peaks, valleys and energies can and will go. In essence it is still about the DJ and what they are feeling like playing, even if that DJ is sensitive to the energy present.

I've been to a number of events where the DJ left feeling like it was the greatest thing ever, that they really felt the energy and worked it, and "wow, people were really grooving." And in truth, in talking to the people there throughout the nite and after the event, there was an undercurrent of dissatisfaction that it just wasn't what they were "feeling" like dancing to. Because it's all that was offered, they stuck it out and made the best of it. It's easy to see how the DJ could think he had done such a good job serving the people: the illusion created was that the people were into it, because they were dancing.

People will dance to whatever is there if they really want to dance, especially if they've already paid their money and all their friends are pretending to be into it too, or if their friends really are into it. I've experienced this far more often than I'd like to admit. The music is barely danceable sometimes, but if the people have come to dance, they'll dance to what's offered, because their "need" overrides everything else, even their concern for the quality or connectivity of the music. And, after paying $10-20 to get in, it's a financial investment and a commitment to stay for some. Have you ever just paid $20 to see some "hot" band and it's not so hot, but you can't get your money back. You've had a crappy week, and you really just want to unwind, you want to dance and so you suck it up, suck down a cold one, and then do the best you can to let go. Usually you'll have an OK time but you never *really* got down, you never *really* felt it fully but the drink helped you get through the night somehow!

In addition, at dances where the music is electronically produced, the level of communicative intimacy possible thru direct spontaneous interactive music simply doesn't fully get birthed as I've experienced it in musical environments where the music is live and everyone is participating in creating it thru their bodies, instruments and voices.

A significant point to recognize here, (and one that sometimes for me is hard to conceive of being a creative spirit who just loves to play all the time) is that there also exists a reality that not everyone wants to participate in creating the experience musically! For the most part, we have not been taught to create in this way. It is foreign and almost always when a group first comes together to try to make music together, there is some amount of chaos before harmony begins to flow. It's not necessarily easy and for many people, not necessarily necessary! Many people find the exploratory process and the "work" in it too hard, too scary, intimidating, annoying or they just simply don't prefer it! So there is most definitely a need for all of it, and it becomes a matter of preference for each person! Again, I would not advocate or suggest giving up one for the other! Fair representation of all creative avenues is for me the ultimate human experience!

Defining Community Music

There are a lot of ways to interpret community music. Some may see it as a concert with a singer, a songwriter at a local café, or a house concert, others as an open mic or a dance party. In my interpretation here, I'm including dance, poetry, song and instrumentation of all sorts, just as the ancient cultures included all parts of the musical experience in their terminology. To clarify further, the American Music Conference provides a very solid definition for "Recreational Music Making" which serves the purpose perfectly! This is also the definition used by most music therapists.

"Recreational Music Making encompasses enjoyable, accessible and fulfilling music-based activities that unite people of all ages regardless of their challenges, backgrounds, ethnicity, ability or prior experience. It is not necessarily or solely about inspiring great music making, nor is it about "performance". It's about inspiring successful living and experiencing the joy of making one's own music. It is not about exceptional performance. It's about fun, personal expression and satisfaction. It's about enjoying the process, wherever it takes you.

Recreational Music Making seeks to benefit the whole person. It seeks to provide access to all those who never thought of themselves as musical and to those who just want to learn and play in a non-pressured environment.

Recreational Music Making does not seek to compete with traditional music instruction. There will always be those who wish to aspire to musical competency and there are the resources already out there that provide these learning opportunities. Recreational Music Making is not about "formal" instruction - it seeks to give people other reasons to make music. The philosophy behind RMM emphasizes that the student is not expected to become proficient on their instrument, but to relax and enjoy the experience of making music. It's about enjoying the process, wherever it takes you.

As referenced by the AMC, "the benefits of Recreational Music Making include:
Fun
Avenue of self-expression
Unites body, mind and spirit
Provides intellectual stimulation
Enhances capacity to cope with challenges
Stress reduction
Opportunities for social interaction and bonding in the group setting
Advances interpersonal communication
Enhances self respect
Allows creativity to shine
Builds community
A great form of exercise
Creative fitness for the mind and body."
AMC: Copyright 2007

Community Music Making is happening all over the country and world in many, many forms from primitive tribal cultures and rituals to group therapy sessions, open jams of all kinds and drum circles in Corporate America. I consider it the original community connection, and one that is irreplaceable for it's benefits to the individual, the community and really the whole human race. There is truly nothing that can replace the experience of being a part of making the music.

Drum and Dance Culture: The Roots of Community Music

As has been previously discussed, drumming has proven to be one of the easiest and fastest ways for people of all walks of life, and ages, to access Music Making. Rhythm is the primary foundation of music, and as such it is the element that most people connect with first: the beat, the groove, etc. The rhythm is what gets us dancing and grooving, and most everyone can tap their foot or hand to the beat of a song easily and without any formal training or any musical knowledge at all. It's practically inevitable really. In addition to drumming simply being the most accessible way to start playing music, research has now shown that there are innumerable health benefits ranging from stress reduction to improved immune function. Neurologist Barry Bittman, M.D. has been one of the most renowned researchers in the field of drumming and wellness. He has done extensive research for many years and his team is credited with many of the scientific and clinical studies that have validated these claims. So, in addition to all of the many social benefits of drumming together, the community aspects, etc., drumming also supports and promotes health and vitality in it's participants! Those of us who play regularly, and all of those who have come before us know this without needing to see the scientific data, but knowing it's there is just more validation to support what we intuitively know and directly experience.

Drum circles have become a place where people can connect with each other. All over the country now, even in small towns, you can find people gathering to play together. It is a movement of people seeking Re-Union with each other and with themselves through a very ancient and powerful way of accessing music and entraining with others. Entrainment is a word that is commonly used to explain the process of connectivity that happens in music. It is truly a universal concept that is found in chemistry, medicine, biology, sociology, and psychology amongst others. It is commonly defined as the tendency for two or more oscillating bodies to lock in to each other so that they vibrate in harmony. It can also be defined as synchronization of two or more rhythmic cycles. An example of entrainment in our physiology is that individual pulsing heart muscle cells, when brought close together after being isolated, begin to pulse in synchrony. Another is the fact that women who live in the same household will often find that their menstrual cycles will coincide after a short period of time living together. The scientific definition of entrainment is a process that occurs in response to naturally occurring phenomenon where the human brain has a tendency to change its dominant EEG frequency towards the frequency of the dominant external stimuli applied to it. In layman's terms, what this means is that humans sharing physical proximity will synchronize with each other naturally. Harmony is a natural phenomenon that happens naturally with humans on a much deeper level than the "conscious" level. Our systems inherently want to cooperate in a natural undisturbed state.

In relationship to music and drumming: this means that many drummers drumming together will eventually merge on the dominant rhythm and play together in unison. This is the inevitable magic of drumming together and is what creates the feeling of unity and connection that drummers feel. Brainwave entrainment has many historical, and often social, manifestations. Drum circles, singing together, chanting, and staring at a fire were all ways that our ancestors partook in the phenomenon, and ways that we are continuing to entrain now even in the modern world.

The drum and dance culture that is alive in the US and western world represents an aspect of folk music that is still evolving from traditional ways into something that has taken on a life and form of it's own. It is participatory, invites a sense of community, and depending on the model, is often totally spontaneous, arising from the moment. If we consider that the integration of many cultures has been an undeniable part of the cultural formation in the US and western culture, we can see how significant this creation truly is. It is a reflection of a need that our modern mainstream culture doesn't address or provide. The fact that so many people in the western world are engaging in these ancient practices either by studying their cultures and learning the traditional ways, or by creating their own experience thru the tools and techniques of the drum and rhythmculture speaks for itself really. There are literally hundreds of regular drum circles listed online and probably countless more that aren't listed that are active as small social units!
There are now groups of people in this sub-culture, particularly the

Pagan communities, that have been meeting regularly for 20 years or more. Their children raised as part of this movement now carry the songs and traditions that this sub-culture has created. Within this sub-culture there are lots of different models, some adhering strongly to a certain tradition such as West African, Mid-Eastern, Indian, etc and some being a blend of all of it with Pagan, New Age, Healing Circles, Arthurian, Shamanistic Drumming, Corporate models and everything and anything you can think of in between. All of these models hold their own intrinsic value and each is a wonderful and valid contribution to creating community thru music. In chapter 9 I will share the model I have created as a synthesis of all that I personally have experienced which goes beyond the drum into the realm of full creative expression thru mindfulness and self awareness.

Moving thru Chaos: Professionals In service to Community Grooves

It seems to me that there is a missing link in the Community Music arena that I feel called to mention: the integration of all levels of musicians. In particular, those who have dedicated their lives to studying the intricacies and subtleties of music, those who we call "Professional Musicians." I personally know of many people who have had all or some part of their original inspiration come from drum circles and/or open community music jams. Some part of that humble experience opened them up to a part of themselves, or to their own potential, or exposed them to the magic of rhythm in community and how it feels to create an ecstatic experience with and for others. It was from that place that they got to where they are now: being paid to perform, traveling all over the world performing with famous or semi-famous bands or as solo artists, with their own bands, etc. I can speak for myself in that drumming opened me up to discovering I could sing, and improv and make songs, etc. I now have recorded 4 CD's, have my own band, and have performed all over the country and world as a solo artist: all of it was inspired by what I experienced in these raw, spontaneous sessions in different communities drumming, dancing and creating together.

A lot of my friends and colleagues who have left the Community Music scene to go into professional music talk about Chaos as a part of what pushed them out and away from wanting to participate in community music making. I can understand, as I am often challenged by it in my work and every time it comes up I have to find a creative way to accept it, honor it and move thru it.

Chaos is a real part of the human experience, and how we deal with it or run from it is also worthy of examination. If we all just run from chaos instead of working to bring order and harmony back from the edge of insanity, then the finer teachings that music has to offer will never be fully transmitted to aspiring players. If all those who master elements of music (in any form) continue to abandon the chaos out of frustration, fear or not knowing how to move thru it, then how can this movement continue to evolve? And, how does that foster strength in community, or teach anyone anything? It may be a bit of a stretch here to say this, but it bears some metaphorical resemblance to letting a child get and stay wild because they are too difficult to discipline. The wild, free abandonment that happens sometimes in Music Making is like the mentality of an undisciplined child who is so joyously lost in themselves and the experience of life that they can't see past themselves or expand beyond their limited perception to consider the efffects of their actions on the greater whole.

I feel that those who have attained higher levels of proficiency and skill could greatly serve their communities by participating and helping to create solutions, modeling different aspects of musicality, and sharing what they've learned instead of just forgetting their roots completely, or running away because it's too hard. This is not in any way to say that they shouldn't step out into their professional callings and become the best they can be in their chosen expression! I just feel called to offer the possibility that by occasionally showing up and holding space in their communities on a more personal and community based level, they can provide a source of deep inspiration, and set an example for what's possible!

In my research, I found an example of this kind of thing in Hungary in the "Táncház movement." "This model involved strong cooperation between musicology experts and enthusiastic amateurs, resulting in a strong vocational foundation and a very high professional level. The involvement of experts meant an effort to understand and revive folk traditions in their full complexity. The movement revived broader folk traditions. Started in the 1970s, Tanchaz soon became a massive movement creating an alternative leisure activity for youths apart from discos and music club: or one could say that it created a new kind of music club. The Tanchaz Movement spread to ethnic Hungarian communities around the world." (Milun)

Inspiring a movement is a pretty exciting concept to me personally! I'm in! Imagine what could be inspired if the professional musicians actually returned to their roots on occasion and offered themselves in service to the community in a way that wasn't about "Watch me perform" but was instead about, "Come on, let's do this together and see how much we can grow, teach and inspire each other!" The entire group would benefit, and that musician would receive so much love and gratitude for their sharing, and so much respect from their community of Music Making Lovers. I have a network of "Professional Musicians" whom I invite regularly to my community sessions in Boulder. Very few of them have ever come, not yet. I will continue to hold this vision in my heart that one day they'll show up and together we can inspire and show possibilities that have yet to be fully experienced for many people, and maybe even start off a Revolution of music that I've been dreaming about for years, that is truly "For the people, By the people." A musical experience where everyone is empowered to express and to participate equally, where there are strong models of cooperation, listening, communication, dialogue, dynamics, play and mutual respect interwoven into the fabric of the Groove and where even the shyest first time player can feel supported, nurtured and invited by a seasoned pro!

Chapter 7

Creating Community Thru Music Making:

Treating the Symptoms of the Lost Connection

"Grooving embodies the duality of community: individuality made stronger through group participation, and vice-versa." (Farmelo)

"No other art can inspire and sweeten the personality like music. The lover of music attains sooner or later to the must sublime field of thought." (Khan)

"As global communication and urban isolation increase and tight cultural communities wither, musical events draw many different people together and unite them on intimate levels. Entering states of unity through grooving, people are (re)united in ways that television and other media can not recreate (Mander 1978)." (Farmelo)

Jenny's Story

"Being someone that has been an active participant as well as someone that has sat witnessing what occurs, I've seen beautiful things come together thru music making that are difficult to put into words. I guess it's something that needs to be felt as a personal experience. What I do know and can say is that in the moment music making brings out a precious and mysterious quality and essence that nothing else does. I wonder if I might be a mess if I didn't have the music, dancing, drumming outlet available on a consistent basis for myself. And for me just being able to 'get out of my head' has been such a relief and necessary part of keeping my balance and peace in times of stress and responsiblities on so many levels. There is no need for head thinking here. It is all free flowing in the moment space. Never quite knowing what to expect and what will show up, there have been times that I have been in awe. I am happy to have my expectations blown apart.

"Just when I think it's the best, I've come to see that it can get even better. I enjoy the in the moment playfulness that happens. Everyone is there, in thier own space but in the space together too. And they are not anywhere else in thier minds, just right there together to create, to play, to express, to be creative and without any effort. This sort of energy seems to transcend all the other stuff, and quite quickly. What I've realized being in The Muse, is how amazingly profound the opportunity is when an individual or commmunity is in a space of safety, love, support, creativity, spirituality and nurturance... it is like a launchpad for sweet things to open up and come forth. It is of an innocent, healing and inspirational quality. Making music together in this innocence feels very essential, especially in our current times. It is something that I wish I could experience in my everyday life. Once you have felt it, you will know what I mean, and to those that have, I'm sure they would agree. Being in-sync, in-the moment, in-tune in some unspoken way, is so very powerful.

"I would also say that it is as if we are able to break through this thick fog of our daily mundane world and transcend to a higher playing field - so to speak. I feel so many people don't have an outlet that they can safely co-creatively express themselves, that it very unfortunately gets bottled up inside and perhaps for a lifetime."

Jenny Sustello, Boulder, CO

Jenny really touches on a lot of points in her sharing. Jenny is a dear friend of mine, she has a beautiful and talented daughter who also comes regularly to the community music sessions I offer in Boulder, called the Magical Mystical Muse Experience. She is right in that many people don't have an outlet for safe creative expression or meaningful contributions in today's world. It is this same theme that I found repeated in many writings by sociologists. In Chapter 1, I used a quote by the Union of International Associates that makes note of the "lack of opportunities" to participate in relation to the collapse of community in the modern western world. "The collapse in the meaningfulness of social participation and a lack of opportunities for participation began around the turn of the century." This lack of opportunities to participate is as much a contributing factor as any other to the symptoms people are suffering from. TV, movies, and the media effectively keep people in the observor/spectator mindset much more than in the participatory vein of sharing stories, talking, and spending time with each other in meaningful ways. People need to feel a connection to each other and making music together is one of the most ancient and powerful ways of cohesifying a community and building long lasting bonds between people. It provides our modern world with something deeper and more tangible than watching TV or surfing the net and brings people forth from a very isolated existence into a way of being that encourages expression, and playfulness as valid and meaningful. In a world of individualism, it fosters group awareness, models cooperation and creates a model to live by that is authentic, artistic and expressive.

Cultivating Community Thru Music Making

We are in deep and serious need of opportunities to share with others and ways to build deeper community in our culture. The west has become a vast sea of isolated individuals who have become strangers to each other thru a powerful system that teaches fear and individualism on a conscious and subconscious level. It is indeed important to be strong as a single being, and yet it is equally important to know how to communicate and share with each other and surrender our individuality to serve the greater whole of humanity when necessary. Individuality is truly experienced when we bring it into service to something larger.

Community begins inside of the individual, as a way of being in the world. There is a certain amount of personal responsibility that we have to assume if we want to be part of or co-create communities out of our world. Being honest with ourselves, our needs, our vulnerabilities, strengths and weaknesses allows us to move forward with feelings of integrity and authenticity while providing context for the integral aspect of basic human connection.

Making music together, on a regular basis, teaches us so much more than just musical skills. If we use it as a practice, it becomes a metaphor for our lives, and teaches us invaluable relationship skills and community skills that can spill over into the rest of our lives and affect change in not only ourselves, but in our community and in our world. I want to revisit the AMC's benefits of Recreational Music Making here. The AMC reports that, amongst other benefits listed, RMM
>   *Builds community
>   *Enhances the capacity to cope with challenges
>   *Reduces stress
>   *Provides opportunities for social interaction and bonding in
>   the group setting and advances interpersonal communication

In considering what builds community, there is much to consider, and many perspectives on what the most important factors are; yet another set of interwoven factors that all play a part in contributing to the whole. I certainly won't be going into all of those here. However, I will touch on a few thru this exploration of music making as a tool for community building!

Cultivating a Sense of Belonging

"In their singing, clapping their hands, and dancing, the people are united...people unite and dance together whatever the state of their feelings." Even if they hurl accusations at one another in the course of the dance, "the next moment, the people become a unit, singing, clapping, moving together (Marshall 1969:380 in Rouget 1985 [1980]:146)." (Farmelo)

Two of the most common complaints in our culture, and especially in those suffering from depression, anxiety and overwhelm syndrome are the feelings of aloneness/isolation and that of feeling no connection to others. Learning to work together thru making music provides a fun and non-linear way to foster a sense of belonging to something greater than yourself and helps people to find connection with each other. An African master drum teacher of mine once said to me, "If you are playing the drum by yourself, you are not playing the drum. The drum is meant to be played with other drums, this is how the songs are made that the drum sings. You can not play alone and think you are really playing. One drum alone is like one hand clapping."

It is clear that whenever people come together to drum, dance, and sing and share their lives this way, they become more empowered as individuals and as a unified energy. They become more than the individuals playing, they become the musical experience itself. I often tell my students that when we sound like one drum or one instrument together, we have reached something very special. When we can no longer feel the distinctions of each part but instead hear the whole song as an entity itself, then we are playing in harmony and unity. This is something that can be felt, experienced and known on an intuitive level and relates to the topic of entrainment that was discussed previously. It's an inevitability of energetic systems to unify and entrain. Music is one of the most easily witnessed arenas to see this. Musicians know this, something happens when we become merged in the music, all of it blends into one great sound that far surpasses what any individual instrument can be alone. We then become greater than ourselves as we become the wholeness of the music rather than just it's parts.

Community Music fosters a sense of belonging. If it is practiced regularly it builds relationships and offers opportunities for people to participate, provides a social outlet, creates networks of people and allows for an experience that is always changing as the group evolves and grows. Those who play together, stay together! As mentioned earlier, there are communities of people now in the US who have been gathering for 20 years and more to share in these ways, and the commitment to keep it going is as strong as ever!

Witnessing and Learning from Each Other

"Now I know, I'm not alone. For years I thought I was the only one who felt that way. The way you felt. I could see it in your dance, the way your body seemed stuck, couldn't move but something inside was screaming to be free. I didn't know your name, or where you came from, but seeing you, dancing that way, I knew your pain as my own. You too carried the burden that I know as my own. Taking you in my arms, eye to eye, I saw that you knew I was seeing you deeper. Collapsing, we held each other, weeping as the drums moved us forward. Slowly, together we danced the dance of recognition, honoring our pain, honoring the journey to overcome it, and becoming free together. Moving it thru our bodies, together choosing to transform the pain to joy. Thank you, sister of the night, for letting me see you, and for seeing me. Now I know, I'm not alone."
Anonymous Rape Victim at Community Circle

Recognition is a vital piece of feeling like one belongs. "Through recognition we learn about our impact on others, and theirs on us. We learn the ways in which we truly make a contribution and this understanding fosters a deep sense of self-worthiness." (Kammen and Gold) Witnessing is a special kind of recognition that withholds all judgement and response and just simply observes. "Being witnessed helps us begin to truly open to what's happening in our lives. Released from the fear of judgement or criticism, we can start to accept difficult experiences, ones where we might feel ashamed, helpless, inadequate or hurt."(Kammen and Gold) Witnessing can be just eye contact, or a touch, and in our music making context, it can be adjusting the volume of the music so that an individual's expression can be heard or following their movements thru the music and interacting with them subtly or strongly. It can be stopping the music, or starting it, it can be just watching someone dance or play and seeing what they are telling us through their bodies and songs. It can be silence.

The story at the opening of this book is a powerful example of a community witnessing one woman's very intense transformation from a heroine addict to an empowered young woman choosing to allow herself to heal. As she poured out her story, the music and voices and energy were interacting in ways that all said, "We hear you, we see you, we acknowledge you here, and we are with you."

In my experience, this part of Community Music Making is the glue that creates unbreakable bonds between those present. We can recognize ourselves in the reflection of another, and share their pain or joy. Being willing to be truly present to those reflections allows us to see our sameness, while honoring our distinctions and differences. We can learn more compassion when we see the struggles and the dramas of each other's lives coming thru our bodies and songs. Recently a friend of mine was sharing with me about a mutual friend of ours. "I can see in her dance that she is ready to break free, break out. She's been doing the same steps for years, and I've been watching her for years, but now it's as if she's feeling into some unknown place. You can see it in her dance. She's just ready to explode, or implode, I'm not sure which." He could see her more clearly in the dance than any words she could possibly speak. Knowing this woman, I know from conversations I've shared with her that he's right on! She is frazzled to the edge, and to her core, and she has to find new solutions to old problems. She's been stuck, and totally looking for a new way to move forward, and indeed explode is a word I've heard her say quite often. The transparency of our beingness is evident in the dance, witnessed fully by those with eyes and hearts to see.

"There are people who I have stayed up all night with playing music that I've never spoken to that I feel like know me and I them deeper than people I see daily in my day to day life. They've seen me cry, felt me play to their tears, seen me in the highest purest joy, felt me play in that space. They've seen me holding others in my arms as they broke down: I've played for them, and with them. They've heard the poetry of my soul, witnessed me in frustration and been lulled into trance by my hands and voice. Much of what I do in my day to day life doesn't really convey or touch the depths of who I am inside, music does. The people I know from these circles are more deeply connected to me than most people I see day to day. Even if it's been years, and I haven't seen them, when I do, it's like old friends re-uniting and there is an effortless rapport that takes no time or energy to establish. We've witnessed each other fully, naked in the brightest and darkest parts of

the soul."
Journal Entry, 2004 Cheri Shanti

Standing witness to each other is one of the biggest responsibilities we have in life to each other. Just quietly witnessing, holding space, and honoring the process of another individual offers them such freedom and grace, and offers us such compassion, wisdom and appreciation that it has the power to transform us at the most subtle levels and at societal levels. Each person we meet holds a lesson for us, if we listen and pay attention. In addition, everything we have learned can become a teaching for someone else. If we are really serious about cultivating meaningful community in our lives, we have to recognize that we hold a responsibility to educate others, just as we have a responsibility to receive the wisdom that others may in turn have to offer us.

Any group or friends that meet regularly and share life in some way can attest to the fact that there is a natural exchange of ideas, information and wisdom that comes just from being together. Musical groups are no exception. A fascinating distinction to me in the musical context is that much of the sharing happens in a different way, not necessarily only thru conversational sharing but in a non-verbal way that is more experiential and metaphorical than literal and direct. For example, I can learn a lot about how I may sometimes want to force my agenda in a situation where it's just not the right time or place simply by watching the way someone tries to force a rhythm into a place where it's just not fitting. I can see that sometimes it's good to listen more and talk less when I see someone playing a loud solo on top of a singer's sweet melody. The sharing is often deeply metaphorical, and if we are really watching and paying close attention, there is a wealth of wisdom that can be transmitted in just one musical experience. Witnessing each other is one of the most direct ways that we gain information and learn from each other and holds infinite wisdom for those willing to watch and learn.

In addition, in music, we can model behaviors for others without naming them per se. This is like leading by example. If I see that a vocalist is wanting to sing and having a hard time being heard, I can instantly lower my volume on my drum, make eye contact or focus my total attention on the singer, giving her space, and model a new possibility for the other players. I don't have to say a word or get up and jump around in the middle with big hand motions, which often serves only to embarrass the shy singer and those drummers who are oblivious to her. I just consciously create a new model, and like magic, people get it and the next time a similar situation occurs they go right to the new behavior without question because they learned the value of it thru their own eyes, ears and experience. I've found also that modeling behavior gives people a sense of inner confidence and empowerment where they get to consciously choose how they want to be rather than being told what is "right" or "wrong" or directed into the action the facilitator wants. They can see for themselves the impact of the model, and use their innate intelligence to do what serves the group according to their own discretion.

Shared Intention: Music as Ritual

"The sacred interpretation is that ritual is the acting-out of a myth. A myth is a story that tells how things in some past time came to relate as they do, and thus how they ought to relate in the present. Its accuracy as history is irrelevant, what matters is its adequacy as a paradigm, as a model for living and acting in the world." (Small)

"During the concentrated and heightened time of ritual, relationships are brought into existence between the participants which model the exemplary relationships whose origin the myth relates. In this way the participants not only learn about the relationships but actually experience them in action. They explore them, they affirm their validity and they celebrate them without having to articulate them in words." (Small)

Ritual is a process of unifying individuals for a shared intention. It is a coming together that says, "I'm part of this." "A ritual is any step that moves us from our individual experience toward an awareness of how our own life is interwoven with other lives, and with life itself. (Kammel and Gold) We've all been part of some kind of rite or ritual: birthday parties, weddings, church services, sports, dance parties, even smoking are all rituals of sorts. Making music together is a ritual of the oldest kind. In music we give ourselves to become part of a shared experience, we become the experience and allow it fully into our beings.

When I was in India, this was so clearly a part of everyday life. Everyday at dawn the monks played gongs and rang bells; the chanting always started right after that. Soon after, people started to come thru the doors, placing their offerings on the altars before they went off to their day of work. Everything in life held some element of ritual for the people there, and so there was a constant reminder for them that they were all in it together: for a greater purpose than just their individual lives. It somehow reminded them of their own sacredness, their interconnectedness with each other, and God and it offered them a moment to give thanks, ask for guidance or offer their devotion to something larger than themselves.

Making music together provides context for the ritual experience. "To take part in music making is to take part in a ritual whose relationships mirror, and allow us to explore and celebrate, the relationships of our world as we imagine them to be." (Small) There is an intention that is shared to create and each person there is conscious of it, aware of it and in recognition of it. In one community I worked in, we had a ritual of opening the circle that involved blessing those who entered, and maintaining silence for the first 30 minutes so that everyone could align themselves, drop the drama of their personalities and be ready to serve each other and be fully present to the "now." In another group I played with, the heartbeat rhythm was always played at the beginning and ending of the time together to unify us as one heart beating together. It was a simple auditory signal that said "We are beginning" and "Now we're done." Simple acts can become rituals, like coffee in the corning, or breathing before and during postures in Yoga, tucking in your child before they drift off to sleep, etc. In fact, much of life can be seen as a ritual if we choose to acknowledge the sacredness of each moment fully.

Playing music, in and of itself, is a ritual. It invites us to being in a different state of consciousness, an altered state, if you will. It transcends the mundane and offers us an opportunity to see that together we are much greater than we are alone. It invites people to a common purpose and provides a fascinating place to explore our inner mythology and how it is in relationship to our physical world, and others in our lives. It also shows us how we may connect to the Divine or "Spirit."

Communication Skills

Communication is the key to any kind of successful relationship: business, personal, family or spiritual. Obviously listening is a vital part of communication. In addition, we must learn to speak our needs, and express ourselves effectively, without hostility, in order to be heard and acknowledged. Communication skills are also necessary to be able to generate interesting dialogue with each other that is stimulating and invites response.

Music making is such a clear representation of how we communicate. If we pay attention we can see subtleties in ourselves and learn how we communicate and how we can evolve our patterns of communication. We can see where we have a tendency to cut someone off in mid-sentence by our over zealousness, where we may not want to hear what someone is saying because we feel so right in expressing ourselves in that moment. We can see how we respond to someone cutting us off: do we get angry or shut down or just hold steady and ignore it? We can see if we have a tendency to want to dominate the conversation, or if we're really active listeners, caring to hear and honor the voice of another as we would want to be heard and respected. All of this shows up in music making, and when we can look at it, with humor and compassion, we can then discover ways to shift and/or support the shifts of others!

How we drum is how we are in life. How we dance is how we are in life. How we listen or interact with others in music is how we are in life. It is the most direct metaphor I've ever seen. Choosing to see our patterns here in the community music experience can give us huge insights to breaking them and creating new ones. Even better, in the practice of making music, we can create opportunities to try out new patterns of communication in non-linear, non-verbal ways, and this can easily transfer to our daily lives. I've had breakthroughs with issues in a moment thru music that I'd been unable to resolve for years with other methods. Somehow the music transcends some part of our logical, rational mind's need to "understand" it all and gives us freedom to just *be* the new pattern instantly rather than trying to "figure out" how we became such jerks or so insensitive or stubborn! In a moment we can choose the new pattern, re-inforce it thru the music, and then choose to activate it in our lives.

Relationship Skills

"The act of music making brings into existence among those present a set of relationships, and it is in those relationships that the meaning lies. It lies not only in the relationships between the humanly organized sounds that are conventionally thought of as the stuff of music, but also in the relationships that are established. These sets of relationships stand in turn for relationships in the larger world: relationships between person and person, between individual and society, humanity and the natural world and even the supernatural world, as they are imagined to be by those taking part. Those are important matters, perhaps the most important in human life.

"In music making, we do not just learn about those relationships, but we actually experience them in all their beautiful complexity. Music making empowers us to experience the actual structure of our universe, and in experiencing it we learn, not just intellectually, but in the very depths of our existence, what our place is within it and how we relate, and ought to relate, to it. We explore those relationships. We affirm them and we celebrate them, every time we take part in a musical experience." (Small)

In order to be an effective community member or to build community, we have to learn how to be in relationship first with ourselves, and then with each other. In the modern world, with more and more people doing a lot of their communication thru the internet and not thru face to face interaction, basic relationship skills are being neglected. Again, it's where our culture places value, and there is a lot more value societally placed on getting ahead, paying the bills, etc. than in building healthy relationships and in the human connection. This is beginning to shift back, I believe, to a more balanced perspective as it's becoming more obvious thru all the symptoms, neurosis and dis-eases that are emerging that humans need each other. There is a need to know how to relate to one another.

If we are willing to really use it as a practice and as a metaphor for life, making music together teaches us the most basic and the most intricate of relationship skills. Skills like active listening, clear communicating, and co-operation are taught and modeled in Music Making. In choosing to use Music Making as a practice, it offers us a deeper look into the nature of our humanness and existence as well as very refined skills of interpersonal dynamics, conflict resolution, compassion, respect and more.

Listening Skills

Listening is an art form in and of itself. I don't mean hearing, that's a totally different thing. Hearing is a biological function that does not necessarily require our attention. We hear things even if we aren't listening. We don't really get to turn our biological function on or off but we can choose to what level we are consciously engaged in the process. Listening is a way of hearing that requires our attention and intention if we are to be hearing beyond the physical function. Active listening is a listening where we are engaged in the exchange of information. It is this kind of listening that creates the opportunity for healthy and harmonious relationships. If we are making music together, it becomes clear quickly who is listening and who is not. Music making invites those with less experience at active listening to give it a try in a safe and respectful environment.

If we are to create music that is harmonious, we have to learn to listen to each other. We need to learn to not play in competition with another player, just as we wouldn't talk when someone else is talking. That's not to say you can't play simultaneously, it's saying we have to listen deeply enough to compliment and support so that all voices present can be respected and no one person or musical quality is dominating another or creating disharmony. In conjunction with listening, this also teaches us that we can stay in our power while also respecting and validating the empowerment of others.

Working Together

A tight community works well together in all situations and knows that every person within that community is important to keep it going. Every member has a function and a responsibility to fulfill. If someone doesn't carry their weight, the entire group suffers. When it's time to play, they know how to play together. When it's time to work, they know how to work. When there's a crisis everyone gets together to help each other out.

Making Music is just like that! By making music together, we learn that each player is part of the whole. Without any one instrument, voice or dancer the experience is changed. If the bass player suddenly spaces out and starts talking to someone in the middle of a juicy groove, it affects everyone, and the entire groove will falter. Each person has a responsibility to do the best that they can to help carry this bigger energy of the music forth. Sometimes it's hard work, sometimes it's play, sometimes it's chaos. Everyone must be able to know how to work together to resolve the chaos before it consumes the group. And sometimes it's pure magic!

Healing the Symptoms of a Sick Culture thru Music Making

In healing the symptoms of modern culture, music making provides many valuable and important opportunities as a therapy and as a model for creating a new paradigm for our culture. One of the most prevalent symptoms, depression, is often associated with a feeling of aloneness and isolation, as well as unworthiness and invisibility. Community is naturally cultivated thru music making, which helps to lessen the impact of the aloneness and isolation that is common in our lives and contributes greatly to depression and mental illness. Music making provides an alternative to bars, nightclubs and TV which invites people to participate fully in the experience and gives a safe space for an altered state of consciousness that is not created by drugs, alcohol or other intoxicants but by the music itself.

The magic of community or recreational music making is that it invites everyone, no matter their skill level, education, ethnicity, age or beliefs. As such it allows for us to transcend our individual perceptions and move into a greater sense of human sharing. This is one of the reasons why earlier explorers were so touched and moved by the music of the native peoples. This is why music is used in peace movements, social organizing, and also why some times music threatens the status quo or governing bodies. Because it can transcend spoken language, and go right to the heart of the human being, music is perhaps the most powerful tool to transform, change and alter consciousness. When the music is truly, "By the people, For the People," then there is even greater potential for us to come together in other ways. It allows us to help to heal our families, our own fragmented minds and our communities thru true heart to heart sharing in a place where words are not necessarily necessary! Music making builds community thru sharing, witnessing, creating ritual and meaning, teaching relationship skills and modeling cooperation! What amazing skills to be teaching our youth, and our leaders, now and for the future!

Chapter 8

The Magical Mystical Muse:

*Modeling the New Paradigm
thru
Mindful Music Making*

A Heart Busted Open by Grace

Once again I am humbled by the omnipotence of grace and sweetness in my life: such constant reminders, when I allow myself to SEE and feel the truth of what is.

Late at night after this medicine of Music Making, my heart is so open and full with love and inspiration. My body is tired and full, and I want to share it, to spread it around and ignite passion in the hearts of others to play together in this healthy and positive way.

Generations of beings, from 10-60 years old are sharing space together, praying around candles and sharing the depths of the human experience thru this practice. Voices, real human voices, not altered, reverbed and fixed up to sound "perfect" but real true voices of all facets of human expression carrying sadness, fear, exhaustion, stress, joy, goofiness, play, prayer. It's all showing up every week in this practice of The Muse.

I am so deeply moved and deeply touched. I remain in the afterglow of grace.

Dancing candles
Soft burning fire light
Deep haunting voices of every human expression
Joy, Grief, Passion
Searching, Yearning, Knowing,
Ancient Songs of wise beings
My own hands on Skin
Pulsing rhythms I never knew I knew
My own voice met by the voices of others
Passion making the Spine Tingle
Moments of Silence and Hearing the Breath of Each other...
More Voices Emanating from the Ethers
A Man swaying back and forth, his hands lifted,
His voice that of an ancient angel adrift in the room
A woman echoing my song, playing joyfully with our shared spirits
Acknowledging Reflection
Two Young Girls Sitting by the Altar,
One with a feather, one with sage, staring intently into the candles,
Their prayers carrying the Prayers of Peace for all of us

They are learning this Sacred Way
To Share with their own Generation....
A Generation who will need them to Carry the Torch

Deep Respect Emanating from every pair of eyes
We are timeless
Beyond words in our hearts
Lovers in the corner
Fingers touching
Softly embracing before spinning back out to the group.
Wrapped in the arms of Sonic Bliss
Created by 15 beings united in Expressive Alchemy

Tears of Gratitude hitting the floor beneath me while my body is bowed
in deep honoring at the Altar of Our Intentions. Ancient crystals and
stones absorbing our energy: charged by our hearts.

Profound presence of the Grace Of "Now" always present
Humbled to Offer something beyond my self
Humbled to Participate and Witness...

Looking around the Circle at the Joyful Openings of Each being
present I realize that somehow we know each other better now.

We are More than we were Alone...
We are Unified in Intent and in acceptance and Willingness to honor
each other fully thru Musical Expression

Thru Witnessing
Thru sharing fearlessly
Thru honoring the children
Thru Being the Truth of our Selves Together
This is the Change I pray for in our world

Journal Entry, 2007 Cheri Shanti

Paradigm Shift: An inevitable Necessity!

A paradigm is an example that serves as a pattern or model for something. It often refers to an example that forms the basis of a theory or methodology. The current paradigm that we are living in is one that keeps us disconnected, isolated and afraid of each other, and really of life itself. It keeps us swimming upstream and exhausted. The Symptoms of a Lost connection discussed in Chapter 1 are indicators that there is a need, a desperate one, for a new paradigm to emerge.

"The New Paradigm" or "Paradigm Shift" are fairly common terms that are used now in many circles and sub-cultures to represent a shift in our consciousness that will move us from our current state of dis-ease to a healthier, more balanced state of being and harmony. It is the ultimate dream vision for the Cultural Creatives.   The "New Paradigm" model includes community, family, healthier ecosystems and more cooperation at a global level amongst people of different cultures and beliefs. I feel that I speak for many in saying that there is a shared belief or vision that the New Paradigm will allow us to draw upon the wisdom and knowledge of the past, other traditions and our own experiences, and will also require that we consider the impact that we are and will be having on the future in creating our lives, our environments and our technologies.

In the unveiling of this shift, it is crucial that we have a variety of models that reinforce, support and nurture the consciousness that we are interested in cultivating, spreading and sharing while allowing us to learn ways to practice and implement them in our world. We need a vast array of "consciousness incubators" to birth this Paradigm shift effectively, compassionately, gracefully and contemplatively. It seems to me that there should be as many "incubators" for this new paradigm as there are for the old (or more preferably). New models for exchanging goods and services, new models for the family unit, new models for growing food, new models of exchanging goods and services, new models for food, for media, for government (especially for government) and for entertainment and community sharings. Many are already in existence and gaining momentum as "incubators" such as alternative currencies, the green movement, eco-conscious commerce, re-localization efforts and others. They're popping up everywhere because there is a real need and call for change emerging in the global consciousness.

Modeling the New Paradigm thru Music Making

Music making holds such vast possibility as a tool to help shift consciousness and model the new paradigm in community and in our personal lives. In this book, I've barely scratched the surface of the possibilities existing in musical sharings. I've touched on how it is one of the most ancient forms of human connection, capable of holding and communicating the energies of a group of people, creating solidarity and a sense of belonging. I've looked at how music can alter or manipulate human consciousness and how it can serve as a model for building community by teaching invaluable life and relationship skills. As many eras, such as those of the 60's and 70's and the Rave culture have demonstrated, music can also be a testing ground for new thoughts, emerging countercultures and shifts of consciousness. This is really just the tip of a huge iceberg of the potentiality for music to influence our worlds.

There have always been musical visionaries, and in the arena of Community Music Making, I am one of them. I know there are others who carry this seed and hold this vision! It is a vision of shared intent, where each participant is truly engaged with their whole being and where each person is in service to the highest possible good in their heart. It invites improvisational aspects as well as traditional. It is an experience of the "now" where each being is heard and supported. Where each being is given an opportunity to shine and where no one is in charge or dictating the experience over another. It offers a whole re-education on how we work together, play together, and build our world together. The people are leading from the people, from their shared desire to make something truly beautiful and magical knowing that the sum is no greater than the totality of it's parts. And, as I touched on earlier, this vision holds a sharing for those of all levels, amateurs and master musicians of all kinds, merging and sharing their wisdom with those who are enthusiastic and new to the experience. I consider it to be a model for the New Paradigm of Community in these ways.

After a few years of drumming and experiencing the different models, such as the "Arthurian" and the "Anarchist" models, the Health Rhythms model and the typical "Facilitated" drum circle model, it became evident to me that what was drawing me wasn't about the drum itself, nor was it about controlling or dictating the outcome of the energy. The drum is the tool for something much greater. I was entranced by the energy, the people being together, moving together, and experiencing life together. In particular, I was fascinated by the connections that happened when we slowed down and became present to each other thru musical sharings, songs, dances, and stories. I was touched by the willingness of people to share their spirits and be witnessed, naked in their pain or their joy. I was totally mesmerized when voices spontaneously came together and people were singing or wanting to share a poem or a rhyme, totally creating their own song in the rhythm, sharing the truths of their authentic selves with each other!

And then I noticed that I was often disappointed that I couldn't hear softer sounds, songs, voices, etc. because the drums would dominate or play so loud that the singer would stop after a few moments, drowned out, suppressed and unable to compete with the volume of the drums. I saw the guitar player sitting behind the drummers, trying to be heard, playing his heart out, but the drummers ignoring him or laughing at him for being so ignorant or foolish as to bring his instrument, a guitar, to "their" drum circle. I saw the guitar player just wanting to be heard, or the floutist, with such a sweet melody to take us to ethereal realms crushed by yet another wild djembe solo. It touched me deeply to witness these kinds of experiences. We all have this place inside that says: "I want to be heard," and I could see the disappointment and frustration that was experienced when quieter voices tried to step out and were crushed by the loudness of the drums.

I saw that there was/is a need for a circle that honors sonic diversity. One that empowers each person to share in their own ways the gifts and expressions of their soul, and that opens up the same kind of magical space that drum circles do without being constantly dominated by the drummers. A place where drummers are given space to get wild and free and loud, but are alsoo requested to hold awareness, and conscious consideration for other voices and instruments to be heard equally. A space that allows for silence, reflection, and poetry; for the voice of a child to be heard clearly and empowered and a place where people can release their fears and share their joys openly without judgement. Beyond that, I felt/feel strongly that it needs to be offered with more consistency than many of the drum circles I've known, most of which are often annual events, at festivals or retreats and gatherings away from the world's daily grind. My feeling was and is that there is tremendous power and learning ability in any consistent practice. I know that the more consistently we come together, the deeper and more open we can become together. As a yoga instructor and healer, mindfulness is a key component I see as crucial to instill in the intention of the circle: a deep awareness of how we affect each other and our world. It was out of that and more, that I created the Magical Mystical Muse Experience in 2005.

I can remember a conversation I had in 1998 at a circle in NY at a Pagan festival called "Starwood" when an elder drummer from that community told me I was "crazy" to think that people would agree to listen to each other more in a drum circle. He told me that it "would never happen;" that drummers would never be willing to co-operate and tune in at a deeper level than the typical "thunder drum" circle. His premise was that the whole point of it was total freedom, total chaos, and that people would never be willing to give up any of their individual expression to allow space for someone else's to shine. Watching him play, I understood why he felt that way: that was the place he played from, but he couldn't see it in himself at all. His arrogance, as an "elder" who had played many years in the "thunder drum" and "Anarchy" models made him blind to the model he was creating for others to follow.

I am very happy to say, he most certainly doesn't speak for everyone! In my experience, people *are* hungry for a deeper connection than what the "thunder" drum circle offers. Everyone wants to be heard, respected and validated; this is a basic human desire. When people understand that in themselves and then recognize that if they give that respect to others, they will naturally receive it back, it becomes a natural way of being and a fun way to share the music knowing that what "comes around goes around."

The Magical Mystical Muse Experience:
A Mindfulness Practice in Music Making

The model that I use in my work is called "The Magical Mystical Muse Experience" or often in short, "The Muse." I created this model after several years of touring the country seeing what was happening in circles all over the country. I studied and participated in hundreds of experiences that were in the vein of Community Music Making: drum circles, open mics, jams, khirtans, and more. From a combination of all of those experiences I created something that I feel holds elements of each while inviting possibility for yet another evolution. The intention is also to be establishing a model for the New Paradigm we are moving towards that invites a more mindful consciousness into our lives and our actions.

I chose Magical and Mystical because that's how I feel in the world of the Muses, and it's how I experience music. There's an other worldly vibration that permeates me thru music that I can't describe: it's elusive, and profound. It goes beyond the physical, and touches the deepest part of my being. It's as if I'm no longer really fully in the physical, but somehow between the worlds as a vessel, as a conduit for an energy that is greater than myself. Some may call it an experience of "God," I suppose. In that space things come thru me that I can't explain. I've played rhythms that I've never learned with complete mastery, spoken in other tongues and known what it meant somehow. I've known just the right word or melody to help or empower another with no forethought or contemplation. I've experienced the future and the past, had visions, seen other lives and been able to see truths in other people that they themselves were blind to and have been able to counsel and help them heal and transform thru the portal of musical vision. In music, I become a vessel and in that, the experience is mystical and sacred. I become the human instrument.

The Muse and The Art of Musing

The Muse is defined as being a state of deep thought, or as the inspiration that visits us thru the creative arts. It is also defined, in Greek Mythology as the Goddess(es) that presided over the different creative arts of music, dance, and poetry. The muse, for me, is that spirit within us that inspires, and touches the Divine thru the human form and vibration or sound. I use the term "Musing" to define the active verb of the art of spontaneous creation using the Muse Arts of music, dance, poetry, rhyme, etc. In the word "Music" in it's fuller, more traditional definition (which includes dance, song and instruments playing), all aspects of the Muse are honored intrinsically in the word. This makes more sense to me than the separation that western thought has created between them. For myself, I know myself as a multidimensional Muser: I am a mystic, a singer, a dancer, a songwriter, a poet, and a drummer. I feel most complete in my being when I can bring all of myself to the experience. I feel most excited and inspired when I am with others who are also given full permission to bring all of themselves to the experience.

The Magical Mystical Muse is a sacred muse play space that is for everyone, not just drummers. All kinds of Musers are invited, and encouraged to participate in the experience. Drummers are invited and encouraged to support whatever else may be emerging, rather than drown it out. In fact, the drummers have the most responsibility to hold the space for the community's expressions. They are held accountable by every person present (not just a facilitator) and asked to be mindful and conscious of their volume when another expression is emerging that may require sensitivity to dynamics! This requires that they be witnessing, observing and reading the energy of the group. This teaches a heightened level of sensitivity and aids in instilling group consciousness deep in the core of the rhythm matrix.

Each being present is invited to consider how they can express themselves fully while also allowing for the fullness of expression of the other beings present. Each participant is empowered to remind the others by being fully present to everything that's going on throughout the experience. It is both an individual and group practice for mindfulness, mutual respect, play and deep active listening that teaches communication and relationship skills. It requests that you be fully engaged and aware of your ability to influence, shape and direct energy. The Muse requests also that you take responsibility for the ways in which you choose to do so. In this way, The Muse cultivates a strong model for community building, working together, cooperation, respect, listening skills, communication skills and interpersonal dynamics.

It is a deep and soulful practice. Sometimes there is chaos as the group works out it's way of finding cooperation and harmony together. Chaos is a valid expression and holds a valuable place in the Muse which will be discussed more in depth in the next section. Our culture teaches us, if something is uncomfortable or chaotic, it should be "fixed," and hopefully by the "leader," or someone else who knows how to "fix" those kinds of things. We aren't empowered around chaos, we breakdown, freak out, lose it, walk away from it, etc. For the first few years when I was facilitating more in the traditional style of being in the center of the group as the "focal" point for the group, I moved the group out of chaos as quickly as possible, sometimes totally stopping the music and starting again on something more familiar and comfortable. The smiles would come back and everyone was happy again. Now, I let it ride and enjoy the show! Chaos does indeed have a place in Music Making. Personally, it's not the place I want to advocate as staying in all the time, but it has it's place for sure which I'll discuss more in depth in a few pages!

**Distinctions between the Magical Mystical Muse
and a "Drum Circle"**

The distinctions, really between the MMMuse or "Musing" as I'm defining it here, and a typical community drum circle, are a short but significant list.

- The Muse may or may not involve drums
- Drummers are requested to be conscious and mindful when vocalists or other instruments are participating and to lower their volume accordingly
- The Muse honors sonic diversity fully: all instruments are welcome, not just drums
- The Muse honors silence as a valid expression
- Poetry, spoken word, and dance are considered equally as important as the drums and vital to a full experience
- Mindfulness and intention are key components in the Muse
- All Participants of the Muse are empowered to be facilitating the experience in moments, so facilitation can shift often based on the inspiration of those present
- Chaos is welcomed and honored as a valid expression
- Therapeutic releases and dramatization, even acting "out" are encouraged

The Magical Mystical Muse is distinct from a drum circle and while drums are a significant contributor, drum circles, in my experience, are a really different,yet equally necessary and valild, experience than a full Muse Experience.

**The Values of Musing and Their Applications as Life Skills
Sonic Diversity: Honoring Diversity in Life**

The Magical Mystical Muse and the art of "Musing" honor all traditions and faiths equally. A Muse is never focused on one particular ethnic musical genre as many drum circles can be (i.e. mostly African drums, djembes, etc.). Instruments from all parts of the world are welcomed and invited equally, drums as equally as stringed instruments, flutes and others thus honoring the intention for Sonic Diversity. Sonic diversity creates an opportunity for us to learn to listen to the subtleties that each instrument and voice holds, thus teaching us to honor diversity in life and in each other; respecting equally all voices, big ones, small ones, loud and soft. It also aids us in learning to listen for the more soft, shy and subtle voices so that we may empower them to share and be heard.

Mindfulness: Self Awareness and Social Responsibility

Musing is really a practice in mindfulness. It is a perfect way to observe and watch how we interact with others and how our actions directly impact the energy of any situation. In the Muse, we can see how it might affect the entire experience and others present in it if suddenly we space out, check out or blast off into a raging tangent of uncontrolled anxiety through our instrument. We can immediately see the chain of reactions that one careless, selfish or insensitive action can cause. Equally we can see what actions based in giving, sharing and recognition create for the group and ourselves. This offers an opportunity to see the responsibility that each person has to do their part to make the ship sail smoothly across any seas. It is also a way to directly experience our impacts on each other. In Musing, an integral concept is that of maintaining a safe, sacred and creative space that empowers each person fully by being sensitive and conscious, awake and mindful in our every interaction.

The metaphors for life in this are many. The impact that our actions, words and thoughts have on influencing the direction of our lives, the lives of others and ultimately the direction that the global consciousness is going are able to be grasped, and immediately received. It gives us a way to see, in the microcosm, how we are all responsible for our piece and if we don't do our part, or do it carelessly or without some level of conscious consideration that there are direct and immediate responses or reactions that occur. It also shows us how we can step up to direct, shift and manifest new possibilities in the moment through our thoughts actions and intentions. When we become more aware of our selves, and our impacts on our immediate environment we can begin to become more socially responsible beings acting with more care and respect for each other. The Muse gives us a lense to look thru, to explore, experiment and examine how our relationships are affected by our actions on all levels.

Equals in Facilitating the Flow: Empowering Equality In Social Action and Respecting Different Perspectives!

Since Musing invites the cultivation of self awareness and responsibility, there is much less of a need for a "facilitator" to stand up in the middle and be the focalizer or director of energy. One of the main reasons I created the Muse in the form I work with, is that I find that when people start to rely on a "facilitator" to work things out all the time, they can become dependant and lazy. They'll often stop really listening deeply and get caught up in the emotional responses that the facilitator is having. Often participants will depend on riding on the facilitators energy rather than tapping in to their own inner guidance. Certainly not always. A truly skilled facilitator, in my eyes, is one who will foster empowered beings to learn from the process while still keeping the energy flowing and empower people to find creative solutions from within themselves.

For circles that meet one time, such as corporate circles, or other large groups of people who have never worked together before in this way, the traditional model of facilitators serve a great purpose and function. For the kind of Regular Music Making practice that the MMMuse is meant to be, the traditional facilitator can too easily become a comfortable leaning post and musical babysitter or director! Having a facilitator there to always be caretaking or guiding the energy gives people a certain ability to space out or check out, knowing that someone will bring them back in line. If chaos comes, the facilitator will work it out, so the participants don't have to and subconsciously they know this. If the rhythm starts to fall apart, the facilitator will pick it up, work it out, or shift it. The facilitator becomes similar to a performer in that they become more or less the focal point of the experience. With a facilitator present, one is expected to remain focused there, to watch them, follow them and do as they suggest or as they lead. Without a facilitator or with an "Invisible" facilitatioin style, people have to be more responsible and more creative on their own, learn to communicate with themselves and find solutions in new ways.

Since a big piece of Musing requests that individuals are self-aware and mindful, there is no real need for a facilitator to jump in the middle of the circle and constantly direct the energy. The facilitator, when present, is there really only to help the participants find their own solutions, not give them to them, not create fixes, not stop or start the flow, but to encourage the flow to find it's own way independant of any one individual's agenda. Each person there is empowered to facilitate parts of the experience if they feel to, and there is no one person who holds more power than another to make those kinds of energetic calls. This teaches so much! It's like taking the training wheels off really. There's no safety switch anymore, and so it offers an opportunity for participants to be empowered as equals and to know when it's appropriate to step in and "direct" and when things can work out on their own without any forced energy. This is an invaluable lesson that has innumerable applications for life and music making! It allows for a more full experience and because each person is empowered equally to request more or less volume, play different instruments, etc. we get to hear and feel the music making thru more than just the facilitator's ears and perspective. The possibilities are infinite and ever changing!

Cultivating Intention and Reflection

Each Muse session begins and ends with contemplative silence. Participants are invited to be become fully present with themselves: to stretch, get comfortable in their bodies and to consider an intention for themselves at the beginning of the session. This can be a personal issue they may want to explore, a prayer they want to embody, or simply to enjoy themselves and find a way to participate fully. At the end of the Musing session, a time is offered for reflection and contemplation to observe the self and be aware of how that intention worked thru the Musing. This teaches reflection, focus, and resolve. It also offers opportunities for empowering the self to follow thru with a set intention and work with issues until they are complete enough that we can see the full circle.

Willingness to Honor Silence as a Musical Contribution:
 Learning the Power of Being

The MMMuse invites silence when it arises naturally. If there is a break in the music, Musers are invited to allow the space for as long as it feels natural. There is no push to fill it, no need to "do" anything. The silence is considered a contribution just as the music and songs are. Movement can still be happening, and often is, so the body can learn the dance of silence in this way. Silence, like chaos, can be the birthplace of creativity when it is honored and allowed to move thru us. Out of the stillness, beautiful magic can emerge in ways that no other experience will allow. In our very busy lives of "doing" all the time, running from one thing to the next, honoring silence and stillness is a forgotten practice. This is a way to allow our minds space for rest, contemplation, relaxation or deeper thought. Allowing ourselves to feel where we are uncomfortable in silence can also be an eye-opening self-experience worthy of deep contemplation. What, in the silence, scares us, makes us nervous, calls us to break it's peaceful presence with our restless minds? What in our culture teaches us respect for deep shared silence? By deeply honoring silence in Musing as a contributing player, we invite sacredness. We invite the "Being" part of Human Being to dance in our hearts, minds and spirits and fill us with an energy that nothing can replace or "fill." Silence heals our neurotic minds and reminds us of deeper realities.

Leaving the Small Talk Outside:
Cultivating Non-Verbal Communication and Comprehension Skills

In the Muse, unlike most drum circles I've experienced, small talk or idle conversation is kept outside of the Muse space. There are several reasons for this. Small talk, daily blabbity blah, "Hey, how's it going?" stuff keeps us in our normal personality state, asks us to respond in certain socially expected ways and doesn't spark up the creative centers of the brain. It is an effective distraction, often, to our deeper truths and feelings. By creating and maintaining a space that requires us to leave the personality, and the normal chit chat that conversation utilizes outside the space, we are inviting something different into the group experience. It doesn't mean that no words or ideas can be used or exchanged, only that the method of communicating break the pattern of small talk and "conversation" in the normal dialogue fashion. The Muse invites story, drama, non-verbal communication, theatrics and spontaneous response that may or may not be direct or verbal. Using rhyme, meter, body movements, facial gestures, comedy, and satirical rampages are encouraged because they give us ways to play out our stories, stresses and experiences in ways that touch a different part of ourselves and others.

Small talk is so prevalent. We spend so much of our day in that space even if we aren't conscious of it. To allow and actually require that we don't go there is a new kind of freedom for us! This teaches us new ways of communicating without words. It also shows us how to see others communicating non-verbally, and offers us ways to deepen our methods for building relationships. It offers new ways of feeling into experiences and moving thru them without the same old same old story and mental run thru of every detail.

Keeping the Playful Inner Child Alive:
Exploring Sacred Play and Staying Young

In a culture and world now that pushes us to grow up quickly, the playful exploratory spirit often dies or withers as we age. Many people have forgotten how to play before they're even 20. A playground offers that space for running wildly in bliss. A safe place for ecstatically trying everything in sight, pushing each other on the swings, laughing, rolling in the sand pit, doing cartwheels thru the grass and busting into laughter uncontrollably. In the Muse Experience, the playful spirit of the child is invited wholeheartedly. Moments of wild, free roaring laughter, rolling around on the floor, doing handstands, singing silly little diddies while dancing around in circles like children do are all totally invited and welcomed. Here, in this sacred playground of the Muse, participants are invited to just relish in their free creative spirits, and let go of the sometimes strangling constraints of being "grown up." Even grown ups need a good romp and a howling bout of senseless laughter if they are to stay young and feel alive. Play sets us free. It reminds us that we are alive and it is in the spirit of youth. Playfulness is an integral part of the human spirit from birth to death. It seems ridiculous that we are conditioned out of it so quickly in our culture and taught that it is silly and invaluable. Play provides us with ways to experiment, release tension and cultivate a joyful life. Musing invites humor and play as sacred expressions of the joy of life!

Chaos: Teaching Coping Skills and Creative Strategy

Chaos is a topic that seems to always bring a snarl to the face of a sophisticated musician or dancer or a bristling of the hair on the back of the neck! This feeling of disgust and "Oh God, not that," seems to just ooze out of people in the presence of chaos. It is often very uncomfortable, especially for trained and sensitive musicians and dancers. However, it is a natural part of the Cosmos, and a natural part of the creative process. Chaos is defined as a state of complete disorder and confusion or as the unbounded space and formless matter that existed before the creation of the universe. It holds complete unpredictability, and for many of us it is a frightening realm that we try to avoid at almost all costs in our lives. When our lives are in chaos, we're swimming upstream, mentally frazzled, exhausted and overwhelmed. Chaos can paralyze us into disempowered apathy where we literally just don't know what to do or how to get out.

If we examine it from that perspective, we can learn it's lessons and use it as yet another tool for transformation and creative expression. Considering this definition alone, there is vast potentiality woven into chaos: chaos as the unbounded space and formless matter before the creation of the universe! To create anything, we need energy! It is truly vital that that energy is unbounded, wild, free and formless so that we can, when we're ready, take it, mold it with our intention and create from that place. Often what pops out the other side of chaos is a unique and magical creation that would never have been possible without giving full reign to the wildness that only chaos can offer! Often I hear melodies that are so surreal, so deeply entrancing and other worldy in the spaces that musical Chaos brings. My body can move in new ways. Ways that it won't and can't be inspired to move when the groove is solid. And when I can truly surrender to Chaos, I give permission to my mind to completely collapse into the unknown and find myself surprisingly feeling renewed and reborn when order is restored. It's akin to having a good deep cry. You know the kind where you just really feel like the entire world is collapsing and you can't possibly go on another moment or day. Somehow after the cry, after the chaos, we gain a new strength, a renewed vitality and a new determination out of the release.

I've watched people move the chaos thru their bodies with such vigor and intensity it's as if they're purifying something, and cleansing their inner realms. Chaos in Musing is crucial in that it allows for us to physically express something that we encounter often in our daily lives and are rarely allowed to validate and dip into without being judged or condemned. By dancing and drumming the chaos, as we do the joy and the pain, we give it a way out of our bodies, spirits and minds. We validate it's existence and honor the wisdom that it holds to teach us. We gain insight into how we can effectively deal with it, transform it and accept it's presence in life without going crazy. If we suppress it, stuff it back, always demanding order and stability, it just keeps being a problem, not offering any solution. There's a great saying, "What we resist persists!" Chaos is very much like that. The more we try to make it better, or "fix it" the more it wants to return again to be allowed it's time to shine. What I've found and witnessed over and over, is that if we don't fight the chaos, and instead surrender to it fully, we have a much different experience of it in our daily lives also. When approached with equanimity and respect, Chaos teaches us lessons that are invaluable to developing fully with maturity and grace.

Chapter 9

Tales of Transformation

In writing this book, I have experienced an interesting journey of self reflection and a deepening of my devotion for this unique artform. In addition, it has proven to be a very powerful way of integrating some pieces of myself that at one point, I had almost given up on. My own transformation thru this way of sharing and being is certainly the inspiration on every level for my life and for this book. I have experienced huge openings and revelations thru music and music making. I came back from the brink of depression thru this magical musical work. I was in a deep state of apathy, where I didn't much care anymore if I lived or died. I have discovered and uncovered many aspects of myself thru this work/play and the transformation that is still happening in me is the fuel for me to share and keep on keeping on. I know there are many who have also felt the power of this way of being in the world whose stories won't be told here, but I just want to say "Thank you" to all of those who have been touched, moved and shifted thru musical sharings. I know that staying present with the Muses, playing with others and building a community of people who love to play, dance, sing and celebrate the journey of life together is what keeps me healthy and alive. It keeps me centered and gives me an outlet when I feel like popping and allows me the opportunity to be as human and as divine as possible simutaneously. Musing has become my therapy and has proven to take me to the heights, depths and expanses of my being over and over again. I am so grateful to share this journey.

The following pages hold personal stories from people who have had their lives transformed thru their experiences of Community Music. Each story expresses a different facet and demonstration of possibilities for us to truly see the world differently when our minds, bodies and spirits are engaged musically. Some of the names have been changed, by request of the contributors. I feel that each story unveils a unique attribute of the Power of the Muse to affect change, heal, support, nourish and unify us.

****

This first story is a healing that was faciliatated through music between a woman and her ex-lover.

"As my body began to warm I found my mind settling down. The music was captivating me. It was something that I had not tried to dance with before. My body moved in new ways: forms of expression that were new to me. I was hearing the call of spirit. It was telling me to fly, to flap my wings and soar above it all. I started to wave my arms as if they were my wings and felt my spirit above the floor. Then it called again asking me to take the mask off so I gestured my hands along my face sweeping the mask away.

"This revealing movement carried me to new states of being. As this state of transformation took place the perceived source of my pain, a man so beautiful, came to me to play in this realm. It was clear from our connection that he was in this state of openness too and together we began to play. We became like angels soaring through the heavens. Dancing without restriction around the room within each other's arms. I was no longer the woman who had been previously hurt by this man. I was a woman of great spirit dancing along side another great spirit. Our light beamed off of one another and our love transcended the pain.

"The music, the movement, and the connection showed me that I could let go and witness the pure potential within all beings. For this sweet night I overcame my stories, my ego and my fear. I was able to devote myself to the spirit within through the form of music and dance. "
Aimee Miller, Boulder, CO

∗∗

This is a personal story of mine from a drum circle at a Pagan festival in Georgia at Dragon Hills in 2001 and holds one of the deeper teachings of my life. It was this night that I gained a deeper understanding of the age old confusion between men and women and it was this night that taught me deep compassion for both genders and gave me the ability to see both sides of a very confusing societal reality which up until then just had me stuck in a place of tragedy and anger. This is straight out of my journal from that night.

"At one point, there were three of them, like wild apes, swarming around her: this beautiful sensual, strong and soft priestess woman. They were all playing hard and wild and I just suddenly began to weep, out of nowhere the tears were flowing. I was feeling anger thru them. Their confused energy: lust, attraction, fear and hatred of the feminine echoed through their intensely loud and aggressive barrage of hits, sending her body writhing in weird spasmodic movements. I felt like I was witnessing a gang rape and it was just making me sick to my stomach, angry and ready to cry, explode, attack them, and run all at the same time. I stayed still, like stone. I felt myself become more fully present, still drumming and holding the space for the circle. My eyes were glued to her body. Watching the way she moved I suddenly got direct insight into her and into many women in the circle's reality simultaneously. It was like a light bulb of consciousness streamed thru me from every woman there and every woman throughout time, and I suddenly saw much deeper than what I was watching. I saw that women have been systematically conditioned to accepting that kind of aggressiveness, non-responsiveness and insensitivity to our deeper subtleties, our softer movements and yearnings. I realized that beyond accepting it, we even pretend, or worse yet, fool ourselves into believing that we like it that way. Porn teaches that, TV teaches it, girl magazines, and media teach it everywhere we look. History holds it too. We've been brainwashed by the whole game of it. We've even been utterly convinced that it's the way it should be, pretending we like it and that it's not violating our feminine selves. I then found myself wanting to play so sweet for her, and to scream at them to back off and leave her alone. I wanted to protect her and all women from this brainwashing we've been subjected to. Instead I took a breath and settled back in for the next wave.

"Again, always observing the inner dialogue, I listened deeper, watching more, knowing there was another level here for me to grasp. I drew forward, leaned against a big djun drum and played with the deepest part of my soul, letting the tears fully come thru me for this confusion between man and woman. I played the sadness and just watched the whole scene, waiting for the next revelation. The tears were landing on my hands, and on my drum, and I cried openly, not wiping them back, letting the whole circle see this if they were watching. I knew here I was safe to take this deep journey within myself and that I would be held in my pain here like nowhere else I could be, without words, without a need to explain myself. I could be in my pain freely.

"I was playing with such perfection and intense speed, and so softly with such tenderness. I knew no one could hear me, I didn't want to be heard, I just needed to play my heart and gain the wisdom I was being given in this moment. A few could see me and I felt a certain solidarity with some of the other women there who I could feel joining me somewhere in this deep inner journey of masculine and feminie.

This whole thing was such a spectacle, these men banging away at this woman whose body was being jerked to and from from the barrage.

"After the tears, grief coursed thru me, deep intense grief. A mourning for that which has been lost, the sweet tender innocence of man and woman together just so shat upon in this world, so cheapened by lust, porn and ignorant conditioning. I suddenly felt the energy of the circle intensify and envelope me deeply. One of my drum brothers came to me, put a hand on my shoulder and said he loved me. Instantly, I was reminded of the love there in that circle. I knew that everyone there loved me. I realized then the other piece I was to be getting that night: men too are doing all that they know to do. They too have been conditioned, brainwashed and deceived by and about the feminine. Those boys weren't playing at her out of hatred, or rageful vengeance towards the feminine, but out of a confused sense of what they thought women liked. They too are victims of the same confusion and brainwashing that our culture has given: that of being hard and fast with women, that that's the "way they like it." Their conditioning is reinforced when the confused females respond, dance, and seem to even enjoy this way of being. The whole thing is confused by itself at this point in time.

"My heart spilled open first in such deep compassion, sadness, grief, and then in joy and awareness. I remembered in an instant my own personal commitment to stay in the light that night, and instantly pushed the energy to another whole level. Calling the energy away from the dancer thru my hands, I stood up off the djun and let these hands that were playing so fast and tight and soft go to the extreme and explode into the Compassion that was in my heart and soul. Those same boys came to me instantly, one on one side screaming "Go Cheri," and another on the other side anchoring down the bottom for me, vibing and encouraging me to ride high and free on the waves of this new understanding. I learned a new level of relaxing into rhythm that fast and sank into one of the most profound jams of my life with a new reality of Compassionate Understanding for every man and woman in my life from now to eternity.

"I saw flames and demons dancing in the fire, and I consciously rode right thru it into the heart of the lotus where the Divine Feminine sat on a lotus blossom with her loving heart. I and the Divine were one beautiful entity of peace. Looking around me I knew I was surrounded by every aspect of the light and the darkness too, and realized this nite was a landmark on my Spiritual Warrior training. From then til dawn it was pure ecstasy. I felt I was making love with the whole circle. I felt my root chakra so open and alive blasting right thru the crown and truly felt completely blessed into ecstasy. I knew that somehow my world was transformed forever."

Cheri Shanti Journal Entry, 2001

****

"In this community music space, everyone was so open and compassionate. There was no room for judgments in this place. As I saw this, I relaxed into the atmosphere, into the waves of music that were speaking to me, through me. My body started moving in ways I never knew it could. It felt like something was moving through me. I was weightless. I surrendered to the safe space and the energy that merged with me. I allowed myself to let go and feel the light of the music, lifting my arms, moving my hips and floating away, yet feeling the Earth more than ever. Some witnesses there called it kundalini. I hesitate to verbalize it because it's so precious to me. I dance now sometimes because there are no words to justify my processes."

Hannah, Boulder, CO

****

"As I began to work more with sound, I found that the transformational experiences that had so enriched my life were more joyful and more profound when providing a space for others - a community - to not only experience them myself but to offer these experiences to others as well and to create a space for others to share. I believe some have called this experience entrainment. Whatever it is called, there is something so magical in co-creating a community space or "container" for the group energy input that doesn't exist in other settings"

Mindy Marmon, Boulder, CO

****

"Art, Dance , Music: the medicine of my life ! They have taught me about the divinity of myself , community and the universe. My greatest teachers they have been! My journey with painting illuminated the universal theme of how energy (the unseen world) translates to form and matter. Growing up in a world of chaos, drawing and painting helped me ground that energy into physical expression giving me a way to reach out and connect with others . As this experience grew in my adult life, my painting took me into live performance art and group mural projects, the communal aspect of art became so much more interesting. The more art became communal, and took shape as movement, the more I could not deny my longing to dance more, and more. As I danced layers of trauma unraveled and the clarity of my devotion to a life of service through expression became more clear

"In the midst of this clarity I had a major head injury. At this time I regressed into the complete chaos of my youth. I was unable to access my healing through dance and my dance community invited me to dance with them by joining the drummers. This is where my life long curiosity of drums and music took root. I learned to dance in the stillness, to be the music that moves the dancer. I re-wove the two sides of my brain back together in the loving support of my dance community and with the oldest healer on the planet: the heart beat. That is where I started. I could only play a heart beat: right than left. Again and again and again, repeating the primal rhythm that would heal my broken heart , body and mind all in one rhythmic journey. The drummers who held me with them as part of there troupe became my mentors, they invited me slowly into building upon my heart beat and we wove the rhythms into the dancers. I watched the dancer closely. In my stillness I was dancing with them and I was healed by their expression, by their freedom, rooting deeper and deeper with my drum between my legs into this ancient healing synergy.

"Visions of all time and all culture that have participated in this primal communal relationship visited me in my dance on my drum. When I was able to join in the dance with my whole body again I was a completely different dancer. I had a new understanding of linking in with the energies of the dancers around me. I felt the fullness in the stillness and moved in it as a fish does through water, dancing with the space and the molecules all around me,

"My gratitude for life, for community and for this initiation into the ancient healing circle of drummers and dancers is eternal. It continues to guide my life."

Ixeeya (Stephanie beacher) Ceremonial dancer, artist

****

The following is a sharing from a musician who, in the context of his performance art, experienced the spirit of community music by inviting the audience to participate.

"Ah, sweet nectar of the gods! Every musician has an occasional performance that transports them into the realms of the divine. It's what we artists live for, isn't it? And these times make up for all of those hum-drum performances when either you or the audience just didn't seem to be working.

"Most of the performances by our band, Stella Luna, fell squarely into the category of divinity manifesting itself through music. Who can say why these things happen? We certainly set our collective intentions before the shows, and usually wound up inviting that particularly intoxicating blend of chaos and magic, occasionally manifesting trouble and illness in the process. Or, as I put it at the time, "summoning the goddess is all well and good, but what are you going to do with her when she shows up?"

"Stella Luna grew out of the Northern California drum circle community in the mid 1990's. A group of us often played on the sidewalks of University Avenue in Palo Alto, encouraging passers-by to join in. The rhythms we generated were often fairly hypnotic, and often went on and on until most of us collapsed. We'd rest for a moment or two, until someone began a new rhythm, and the rest of us would start drumming again. We were joined on more than one occasion by a didgeridoo player or two, and at those times, things got even more trance-inducing.

"From time to time we brought elements of ritual to our shows. When we found ourselves playing on Ash Wednesday, I brought ashes to the show thinking I would, at an appropriate moment, smear them on peoples' heads. I thought maybe a few people would go for it. I wound up smudging virtually everybody in the room. As I looked into their faces, I didn't see the sense of irony I was expecting. I saw a genuine desire for a communal spirituality. Even among the dis-enfranchised punks and gothlings of San Jose, there was an overwhelming urge for somthing spiritual.

"At another show—or maybe it was that same Ash Wednesday performance—we somehow finished our set sitting outside Cafe Leviticus on the sidewalk, along with a good portion of the audience. We all sang together in a beautiful and spontaneous drone.

"Another performance ended with the audience following us outside to a pedestrian tunnel that ran underneath Alameda. It was spontaneous, unorganized and fairly chaotic. We were doing our drumming thing, but as the evening wore on, we eventually wore ourselves out. Each of us (unbeknownst to the others) handed our drum to an audience member. When I looked around to find my band-mates, none of them were playing. The audience had completely taken over, in the best possible way. "Thank you, everybody," I said, when things finally died down. "We're Stella Luna, AND SO ARE YOU!"

"At the peaks of these Stella Luna performances, when band and audience merged together in loud ecstatic bliss, I am reminded of the words of Chogyam Trungpa: "At that moment, everything we see appears to be beautiful, loving, even the most grotesque situations of life seem heavenly."

Neville Harson, Boulder, CO

****

"I once attended a gathering where we journeyed as a group. After the journey, my friend, a beautiful wise woman, shared that sometimes we are drawn to things that may not be easy for us, but we feel compelled to them anyway. She mentioned that this may be because our spirit helpers and companions really enjoy this and because they are spirits they need to enjoy it through us; that perhaps sometimes they get bored with us when we are constantly working and studying. So right then I realized that my helpers must love to dance, and they must love music, because I struggle with expressing myself through these, but I am so attracted to them. It's a new inspiration for me to let go of my ego and play and dance because it makes my companions happy."

Caroline Lee, CO

****

"I started drumming when I was maybe 7 or 8, and I still drum now, so of course community drumming has been a major transformational force throughout much of my life.

"I suppose could talk about the microcosm within the macrocosm I perceive in various community rhythm experiences, and how my interactions in these circles have helped me to refine my interpersonal skills both in and out of the circles.

"But I could also talk of the nanocosm within that microcosm that I perceive within myself while participating in community rhythm events- and how this has allowed me to transform my relationship with myself, and consequently, to just about everything in my life.

"This process has been most clear to me in my experiences in regularly attending TaKeTiNa circles over a period of years. I've seen direct, concrete changes in my self-talk, and all that flows from that - as a result of my participation in these circles. I've seen this in all rhythm/music circles, including the beach jams and the alchemical fire circles,where inevitably my 'stuff' comes up and I have an opportunity to witness that and maybe even let it go."

Tara Severns, HI

****

Feet pounding earth
Hands on skin
Blessed bliss in rhythm's kiss

Earth child
Mother of All
I am
Graced with the blessings of the honor to drum
To be called to that ancient portal of power and service..

In the circle
The firelight glows
In the rhythm
Everything shows

Many are here
But few will see
The truth behind the masks
We wear in society

Repressed anger
In the way that man hits his drum
Violence unspeakable
Unconsciously displayed

Love and wonder fresh and new

In the rhythm, we can see what is true
In the circle, we share it all
Me and you.

Cheri 2002

****

"From the very beginning I loved making 'drum music' with other people. Even though I spent hours alone with the drum practicing technique and having powerful musical experiences, somehow with other humans it was always a bigger buzz.

"I started by playing Djembe in two and three drummer combinations thus playing two and three parts simultaneously. Drum music is such cool music. The overtones or the extraneous tones that are produced from it are fascinating and quite often different experientially for each drummer involved. I've personally heard flutes, vocal choruses, orchestras, and single voices singing or chanting within the drum music. One of my senior citizen drummers (82 yrs. old) hears, what he calls, Tibetan Monks chanting every time we do a drumming meditation. It's what actually intrigued him to continue drumming and ultimately purchase a drum and play it at home. He never misses our weekly class/gathering: it is still his favorite way to drum. So we also connect with parellel communities.

"Soon, I started teaching the djembe drum to anyone that would listen to me. I even provided a drum...I was intently looking for people to drum with Yes, I had basic selfish ulterior motives! .I devised a method of learning rhythms and technique that turned into my teaching curriculum. All I had to do was stay one rhythm ahead of the 'class.' It was basically "come practice with me!" However, that's where the realization that 'practice is meditation' came to me. When a rhythm is repeated for 5 - 20 minutes it becomes a mantra that leads to conscious or un-conscious meditation. The cells know it no matter what. Upon discovering this, I rubbed my hands together and said, "Hmmmm, what a great way for people to gather and meditate!?!"

"So. I've been creating drumming communities thru teaching classes that give just this experience: the 'drumming meditation' experience. A sitting meditation for people who can't sit still!

"I drum with senior citizens, people with alzheimers , children and lots of us older children pretending to be adults. Some of them are community drum circles, others are classes that teach specific rhythms on specific drums. All the combinations lead to the same effect: a sense of well being and a community experience. It gives us a space to be kids again while remaining inside of ourselves. And there are many health and therapeutic benefits. Many of them that were speculated 10 years ago are being corroberated by medical science and science now.

"Group drumming is mighty powerful and those that have partaken become firm believers and continue to drum in their lives. Many become facilitators and/or hosts of drumming circles. At the very least they become 'drum circle junkies.' It is indeed powerful when humans gather to make art and music. Drumming happens to be an all-inclusive activity.. It always puts one in the present, in the 'now.' If 50+ folks are all in the 'now' having and doing love-based thoughts and actions: what could be better? 'Tis a powerful use of space and time."

Greg Hansen, Boulder, CO

****

"I lost my mom and 7 siblings to fear in 1999. They bought a compound with lots of provisions saved because they thought the end of the world was here, became extremists and shut me out. I lost 5 sisters, 2 brothers, my mother and her 20+ grandchildren in this ordeal. They lost a son, a brother, and an uncle that had lots of love and life for those around him. I never imagined something this bad could happen to me. It did. I believe that people in sorrow or fear have no use for happy people around them. This being very tragic in my life, it's far behind me now, though I can't even begin to tell you how much it hurt. We still don't talk even though it all fell apart on them. Their pride and my happiness will never allow things as they were before fear.

"I know for a fact that dance helped me through this and I would not be as happy with such a great loss, if I didn't DANCE!!!"

Anonymous Offering

****

"Through creative expression I have realized my purpose as a co creator of heaven on Earth. It is also through creative expression which I manifest this purpose. When I am create, I accept this mission and my true essence.

"My relationship with art though out my life has opened me up to understand the profound healing abilities of art. I spent the better part of eight years of my childhood in an ice skating rink as a performer and competitor. My creativity later manifested through Visual Art, giving me the inclination to become an Art Therapist because it was through creative expression that I let go of many different levels of emotional and physical pain.

"I have experienced healing and transformation through many art forms including painting, writing, sculpting, installation work, writing, dancing and now drumming. We are very fortunate in our community in Boulder, CO to come together in our own individual energy as a part to the whole of working together for transformation. As a channel of music through dance in some of the gatherings I have experienced some of my deepest realizations of self.

"Dancing allows me to pray, to heal, to give thanks and transcend. Movement and dance is a tool to enable light into my body and enter into that deep place of healing by becoming fluid in the imbalance. It is a tangible way I and others assist Earths ascension into higher dimensions because it is possible to create such movements with our body and energy. I am both grateful for and long for that place where I am grounded in my body while soaring in the ethers. The place where I surrender to my soul and magic happens. It is here I am home.

"I have had the opportunity to experience Community music at Cheri Shanti's Magical Muse, Gypsy Nation and Dance Home now to name a few. The combination of intentional energies with one another in such deep intimate space creates healing not only on individual levels, but greater global levels as well. This sense of community is unfolding more and more. I have watched the community come together with such genuine support for each other and ignite the excitement of each of our personal creative process. I allow myself to be amazed at our unity as well as the truth of my souls own personal healing process, and the power of the great spirit moving through me. I am honored to be a co creator of this evolutionary time.

"All of these creative tools of the Arts and Muse Arts allow us to resist that mind chatter that we have been conditioned to accept. They allow us to grow individually, heal our souls and heal others. Creativity enables us to remove obstacles, judgment, self doubt, and the sadness of Earth's present condition because we are taking action to reshape the world into one of more love and light. In specific it is the community gatherings and combination of so many unique and beautiful energies and various forms of expression which create such high vibrations of peace and hope. The support and love is like none I have found before in any of the many communities I have been a part of. It is new and exciting and allows me to access the depths of my soul. It is here I can uncover my deepest wounds and dis-member my self in order to remember the deep essence of the truth I am. I am amazed at the light coming through our community and feel great joy to watch others become surprised at the extent which we allow ourselves to grow. As I have been guided to know my healing exists on many levels, I want to spread this very concept far and wide to help others see the transcendental possibilities of healing through the creative arts. That repressed emotion may arise from the caves of our hearts to transform from fear and stagnation into love.

"In past service work at a hospital doing art groups I have used art as an outlet for terminally ill children, so that they may forget their very surroundings and condition and become fully immersed in artistic outlets. My current service work at a youth shelter in Boulder continues to remind both myself and the teenagers to come back to that peaceful place of somber creation. In the future I want to hold creative space for those in pain because I know the effects and I have personally found my deepest healing through the creative arts. I feel the combination of mediums and art forms (visual, movement, music,etc.) is profound and I want to share the light I have found through creativity with those searching for that missing link to their bliss."

Lauren Clark, Boulder, CO

****

"When in California at a middle eastern drum festival, I was drumming with the circle and started to hear more than there was. I could hear the calls in the market place as vendors hawked their wares. I could hear a man singing in an arabic language although there were no men singing in the room where we drummed. The best part was the feeling of being there. I could hear the voice through my drum, I could feel the kinship of those around me in the bazaar and I felt as though I were at home albeit, in a very far away and long ago place. It has to be one of my favorite memories."

Jodi Connely

****

"Community ecstatic dancing offers me the opportunity to express my creative self at both the physical and spiritual level, in a very real way. Or perhaps I could say that Creative Energy expresses itself through me as I yield my body and spirit to the Dance. As I surrender, the Dancer within emerges, and my body cooperates with its impulses. Somehow I just "know" how to organically move my body in a way that synchronizes with the tone and message of the music, and with other dancers. (At least it feels that way to me.) I feel one with the music, one with other dancers, and one with my innermost self. Sometimes it even feels like I am dancing a story or a journey. Gone are the old dance club days where I awkwardly try to string together some jerky moves that I hoped looked cool to others. In that unnatural mode, I always felt timid, self-conscious and inhibited; there was no power or aliveness; and there was nothing organic or spiritual about it. But in the safe, nurturing, and open spiritual environment of the ecstatic community dance, I feel God-conscious and uninhibited; I feel powerful and alive; and nobody cares how well I am dancing or what I look like. It is simply unbridled, rejuvenating, healing FREEDOM! And, it's a great workout!! Surrender to the powerful Dancer that lies within you by not caring how you look to anyone else on the dance floor: this is the key. Oh, and by the way, I am an engineer by profession who has no formal dance training."

Ed Villano, Denver, CO

****

"I've been both musician and dance-a-holic since age 14 at least. Now I'm 64. Yes, I've frequently lived and worked with others who don't seem to undertand. They thought I would eventually outgrow my "childish" or "adolescent" behavior. But I never did outgrow my need to regularly wash my soul clean of extra baggage. No, I never did outgrow my need to connect with and know my fellow dance lovers in deep non-verbal ways that allows me to feel a trust in my connections with them which runs deeper than any written contract or verbal promise could ever allow. Yes, I danced through the decades of raising kids and I took them with me to learn the arts of sacred playfulness from an early age. I danced through the romances and I danced through the breakups. I danced out my sorrows and I danced out my joys.

No, I never took a single "dance lesson." But I'm always there ready to keep dancing and I'm blessed to be in a community where I am surrounded by other dance-a-holics with whom I have now been dancing for well over thirty years. We've danced our way through thick and thin and now well into a healthy "old age." We'll see how it goes from here on out!"

Cameron Powers

Chapter 10

Awakening
your
Authentic Inner Muse

"People of color, people of all classes, both genders, have been systematically musically incapacitated." (Small)

"Learning to play music, as an adult living in the modern world, has been one of the greatest gifts I've ever allowed myself! In making music I am so alive. I am in touch with a part of myself I had forgotten existed. It doesn't matter how good I am, or if anyone likes it, I play now for myself, for my own sanity and to let out the truth of my existence."   Anonymous

I want to revisit a quote I used earlier in the book here, "There is a critical loss of music making going on that is not 'natural' or 'inevitable,' nor is it natural that just the 'talented' few are doing something and the 'untalented' many are applauding." (Keil)

Making music is so much more of a natural phenomenon than we have been taught in western society! It's not this "far away" concept that we can't reach or grasp as it's often portrayed to be, and, as mentioned in Chapter 2, you don't have to study theory and practice for years to be able to play and participate in making music! If you believe that music is just for "musicians," you've bought a lie! It's false programming, plain and simple. Music is for everyone, and everyone has music inside of them. "The taste for music is inborn in man, and it first shows in the infant." (Khan p. 52)

Now, if you want to be the world's best classical pianist, or a ballet dancer, then you'll have to do some studying, competing and dedicate your life fully to practicing and evolving your art. To just enjoy the simple pleasures of sharing a groove with others, you don't need to go to school, take a class or study at all if you don't want to. Of course it will help you to learn some basics, but it's not absolutely necessary! Remember, I'm considering dance, poetry, rhythm, melody and all aspects of the Muse when I say "Making Music." There are so many valid musical expressions, and from what I've seen, every person holds an innate ability, it just manifests in different forms thru different vessels. Some may just feel it, naturally, in their bodies. Some may be inspired in their voices to sing or chant. Some feel it coming in their hands tapping or foot stomping; some in words or stories, or poetic inspirations etc. In expanding the definition of "Music" we honor that each individual has a unique expression (dance, song, poetry, music,etc) and that all are part of the greater whole of Music!

There is something in music that keeps us alive. Some of the healthiest, most vibrant elders I have ever seen are avid dancers and/ or musicians. They radiate joy, and youth and they possess this infectious passion for life that many people their age and younger have left behind years ago. Many of them, when asked, have said to me that it's the Music that keeps them alive and young and so they dance and dance and dance, and they just keep getting younger! Music is passion, it is life, and it is such a profound way to keep saying "Yes" to life!

So, here is an official invitation to those of you who are feeling the groove inside you but have been afraid to let it out.   An invitation to those of you who hear a little didee but are too shy to sing it, and tothose who feel the beat and your dancing feet are wanting to step out but you're afraid for some reason: Come on out and play! It's never too late, and you don't have to want to be a rock and roll star to enjoy making music, dancing and exploroing your own Inner Muse! This chapter is for you: to encourage, inspire, and invite your Muses to move thru you in whatever ways they want to. This chapter is inviting you to start taking baby steps towards creating a life that sings thru you, dances thru you and inspires others to do the same! Whether you've played before or not, this chapter will offer you a few considerations on your journey to bringing your authentic Muse to life.

 Do you know that it is already living in y ou, and always has been? It's just waiting for you to give it a chance to play through you! You were born with it and it can never be taken from you! Your Muse is so unique: no one else can say, feel, sing, dance or express *your* muse in quite the same way that you can! So give Your Muse a chance, allow it some space to be heard, to be felt, and give it a warm invitation to the dance of your life. You may find at times that it is sad, even mournful, and depressed. You may find that it's be-grudging you all the time that you left it sitting alone in the dark corners of your heart, but with the tiniest invitation, the softest whisper to come play, Your Muse will jump to it's dancing feet and respond to you somehow! Your Muse wants to be recognized, seen, felt and expressed, just as "you" the personality does. So let it sing the sadness, let it dance the grief, let it slam out it's resentfullness and anger thru dance or drumming until it's returned to joy or quiet emptiness!   All the emotions you can feel, Your Muse can express for you! All the pain, all the joy, all the sorrow, all the vitality, all the fear for our world, all the loneliness and isolation: All of it can be transformed, and experienced thru Your authentic inner muse!

So, if you're feeling unsure about where to start, you will find some insights here! This chapter is your invitation, your hand in the dark to pull you up and a playful and realistic approach towards inviting your Muse back into your life wholeheartedly. I hope this chapter helps you to gain some insight into ways that you can start to overcome your fears, move thru your challenges and find your Authentic Inner Muse, your own funky groove, your song and dance to share with the world and bring to your community!

Muse Lost but never forgotten!

My mother was a world class Hawaiin steel guitar player in the 1950's. My uncle, her younger brother, tells me stories about her that are just amazing to me. They are stories that make me want to cry with pride and grief simultaneously for her and for the part of my mother that I may never know. He tells me she would practice for hours, even in the freezing cold winters, alone in her room with total devotion and patience. She was in a band in highschool, and every other band around wanted her to play with them. She was even teaching others at a very young age before she went to college at 18. She played at all the local fairs and was renowned as the "best" in the whole region. And to top it off, she was one of the few female musicans of her time in Maryland who actually got out there and made a mark in her community, performed and was empowered enough as a musician and as a woman to be respected where she grew up.

I'll probably never know what happened to my mother and why she stopped playing, but she did. And I can tell you, that there has always been a huge hole in my heart that I may never hear her play and that I may never get to play with her! I've asked her many times what happened, why she stopped, and she just can't talk about it. Something seems broken; the memories are too painful for her and she just changes the subject instantly. She wouldn't even show me her guitar until I was nearly 30. I think she only gave in because I had finally pestered her so much she couldn't stand it anymore. She still has it to this day. It's a beautiful National Steel Guitar and probably worth a lot of money, but she's not selling it, she's still holding onto it. My prayer is she'll start playing it again. She won't talk about her playing days, or what made her stop, she never has, and maybe she never will. Something made her stop, something made her give it up and she's never picked it up again. The funny thing is she acts like she doesn't know the first thing about music. I don't doubt that she knows far more than I do about theory and performance, but again I'll never know as she just won't/can't talk about it. I know she knows about music because a few times we've been listening to something, and she'll make a comment that only someone with a musical ear would notice. "What's that instrument?" or "That's interesting music" or some other musical comment has occassionally slipped out if she hears a unique instrument or an interesting scale. I know that inside of her there is a world class musician who's been repressed, shut down, or convinced that it wasn't "important" anymore. Somewhere along the line she stuffed her Muse in a tightly sealed box, hid it in storage and pretended she never had one. I can also tell you, my mother has suffered from depression for many years, and I often wonder if the two are connected. It's hard to imagine that they aren't.

There are many reasons that people don't, won't or think they "can't" play music: fears of being judged, fears of not being good enough, of failure, or even of success, cultural disempowerment and the glamorization of music (as mentioned earlier), oppressive situations or environments that don't feel safe or supportive for creative expressions, etc. Many people play when they're young, and stop when the pressures of modern life start to hit them with families, and careers, or when life gets "busy." There are many reasons that people either don't ever try or give it up, some are really obvious and may seem to be"practical" reasons (like maybe having kids) and others are more personal, deeper and may seem harder to deal with on an individual level. For example, maybe, like me, your sibling made fun of you when you sang, so you got self conscious, like I was for 15 years! Or maybe you had a teacher who scolded you for experimenting, for actually really *playing* your instrument. The spirit of play is, in fact, experimental by nature and that is not always well received by strict disciplinary teachers. Perhaps, somehow that shut you down. Perhaps you've always known masterful musicians or dancers who are "so amazing" that you felt intimidated or "not good enough," so you just never tried. Maybe your girlfriend or boyfriend would get frustrated trying to dance with you and said you had 2 left feet, or you wrote a poem and read it to people and they laughed at you.

Whatever the reasons, many of us have a desire to be musical that gets shut off some where in our lives. Often it is when we are young, impressionable and/or vulnerable to the input of someone we respect or even look up to, a parent, a teacher, a peer or a romantic interest. Sometimes, like with Beth, it happens later in life when we are really seeking a new outlet and needing to learn a new part of ourselves to become more whole.

"Even now I remember it with a twinge of shame, my first drumming circle. It was not long after a divorce had left me feeling unmoored in my life. Trying to pick up the pieces, not knowing which direction to go next, I was allowing myself to try many new things. Singing, dance, and different meditation groups were all part of my explorations. I went to a drumming class. With no introduction, everyone just fell naturally into a somewhat complicated rhythm. I'd never hit a drum before, and I just experimented, having no idea at all what I was doing. "Err, thanks for sharing," was the teacher's terse remark. I felt humiliated. It's one of the few memories that stays with me akwardly, since I generally never mind making a fool of myself so much. I felt really stupid.

"I contrast this with the positive encouragement I received from my kindergarden teacher. When I made the giant leap from scribbling to coloring with my crayon in parallel lines, because the boy next to me was doing it that way. My beloved teacher noticed, and told me I was going to be an artist. What did I know? If she said so, it must be true. So I have never felt a bit of inhibition about creativity in any of the visual arts, from basketry to fine art portrait sculpture, but drumming was scary."
Beth McCormick, HI
Feather and Visual Artist

Beth is one of the most amazing visual artists I've ever known. She does magic with feathers and clay, creating unbelievable pieces that radiate pure mastery, patience, diligence, visionary depth and passion. She was told she could, early in life, and she's never doubted it and she is a very successful artist today!

How many of us might have been more inspired to keep doing art, or music, if we had received positive reinforcement, support, or words of encouragement from teachers, parents or peers? This is truly a significant teaching in raising our children to be successful. Children are impressionable at young ages, and will believe what they are told and shown about themselves because they trust their teachers, parents, and peers. That programming can stay with us for many years, sometimes lifetimes. It takes conscious effort to unravel the stories other people told us, and discover the truth of ourselves as adults.

While I was in Hawaii, I stayed with my friend Morgan, who is the caretaker of the land Beth lives on with her partner, Charles. Hearing this story from Beth really touched me, and brought to mind the many, many students I've had who have been led to believe that they "have no rhythm." Phrases like "I can't keep a beat to save my life," and "I'm a musical disaster,"and "I've got no rhythm," come out of people's mouths often when they hear I'm a rhythm teacher. In my work I have met many beings who were put down, shut down or incapacitated by a "teacher," or a family member or friend. In taking the time to work with those beings, I can honestly say that I've never found it to be true: not once in 10 years of teaching have I found someone who "has no rhythm" or "can't do it." I did a lesson with Beth while I was there, in Hawaii. The truth was that she has perfect rhythm and she is a natural lead player, creative and expressionate. There is nothing wrong with her musical ability at all, she has a very natural solid connection. What may indeed be true, is that the "teacher" couldn't do it! Perhaps that teacher who shut her down just didn't know how to deal with a truly creative being in his class, or was threatened if a student was playing some lead and accenting the rhythm in a new way, or perhaps he simply wasn't capable of teaching someone who maybe had a different learning style, needed a little more time, energy or support, or possibly had a few more years of "I can't" programming to get through. Often, particularly in some of the more "traditional" teachings, there is little patience for deviation and these "teachers" would rather not be bothered with someone who might just need a different approach or have a more unique, expressive and creative voice. Sometimes "teachers" can get caught in their role and lose the ability to release their ideas of right and wrong to be able to provide a safe and open space for different learning styles, creative spirits and the unwinding of old programs.

The thing to know is that *you can*! If you want to, you can! That's all it takes to start finding the Music in you and your own authentic inner Muse! You just have to want to do it and be willing to step out and try! It doesn't matter if you are someone who has put the music aside, or if you gave it up, thinking you "outgrew" it, or if you are someone who has never even tried to dance, play, sing or get in the groove. Just let yourself try, you might indeed be surprised what's in there within yourself waiting to be set free! Be patient, and have no expectations and just enjoy what comes as part of yourself and honor all pieces of the puzzle as they begin to unfold!

Give yourself a Chance!

Let's imagine you're interested in learning to swim, and you have a dream of swimming across the ocean. The problem is you've never swam before and let's even say, your mother always told you "You'll never be able to swim, you're like a log, you'll drown, sink straight to the bottom of the sea you will!" You live in Iowa, have never even seen the ocean, and you, in your total acceptance of your mother's words, have managed to avoid even taking baths. You've never been to a lake or even a swimming pool, but still you have this desire to swim across the ocean; you dream about it constantly. My guess is, it wouldn't be a wise choice to get dropped off in the middle of the ocean from a helicopter on a wild stormy day and "go for it." I mean, you might survive, you might even learn to swim really quickly, but then again, you might not. You might panic, flail and possibly drown. If you did survive, you may have to be rescued and end up having a big fear of ever doing it again because your first experience was so traumatic.

I know this is a silly metaphor, but I feel like it's a significant place to start! If you want to open yourself up, it's important that you find a safe, and empowering way to begin your process. I'm not saying you need to take lessons or take a class, though that is one possibility. I am saying that splashing around in the tub could be a good start, go visit the local pool, get in and splash around in the shallow end and acquaint yourself with water a little bit before jumping in to swim the seas.

If you show up at an open mic at a local bar with a brand new drum or guitar you just bought at the music store that day, with a big smile on your face, and try to sit in, again, you might survive and even learn some things, but you might also leave feeling a little bit inadequate or confused that the bass player kept giving you funny looks, and the drummer kept yelling "One," at you. You may even feel so discouraged you won't try again. You've got to walk before you can run! It applies to everything it seems! You CAN do it, but like anything, it's a step by step process. Your first steps, like when you were a baby, should be careful and preferably with someone there to hold your hand or atleast pick you up and let you know it's OK, everyone falls sometimes, so now get back up and try again! When you make those first steps slowly and gently and then you *don't* fall down and crack your noggin, or you are encouraged to get back up when you fall and not scolded, you will want to take more. You will believe that you can take more! These first steps are also a huge piece in learning about yourself. Music is such a powerful way to get to know yourself and if you spend some time cultivating a relationship with yourself in this process, you will find that you will not only be ready to swim the sea faster, but you will be an inspiration to others to come and join you! You will set an example of possibility with perseverance and conscious actions!

Community Music spaces such as the MM Muse and open community drum circles are the perfect opportunity to start exploring your Muse. They are safe havens and you will find yourself supported, empowered and acknowledged every step of the way! They are created just for this purpose of discovery and unveiling. They are all about the processes of sharing and exploring our creativity together and you can learn a lot if you use these times for going deep into a self study practice within the safe space of the group! Utilize what is available to you in your own community in the form of community music jams, improv sessions or lessons or some combination of all of it. Look online or in your local community mags for events happening near you, or better yet, invite your friends over for your own community jam!

Finding What's Natural

I have a friend whom I've witnessed for several years in the drum/dance community. He loves to drum. He really wants to be a drummer. He's taken classes from African masters. He has studied and knows this and that rhythm and he practices a lot. His commitment touches me deeply as I see that he is working with something inside himself that is very deep. When he sits down to play, it's hard to explain, but it just looks like it's hurting him. What comes out feels forced and contorted, it just doesn't feel natural in any way really. It's not so much about how it sounds, that's not even relative in this context, to be honest, it's more this feeling of witnessing something unnatural, forced and uncomfortable. It's kind of like watching a lemon going thru a tube of toothpaste! The drum just isn't natural for him; he openly admits it, his body language shows his own awareness of it and everyone who hears it can feel it energetically. It's not that he doesn't have rhythm, or that he "can't" do it at all. It's just not his most natural expression. Now, when he sings, it's almost the exact opposite: his face lightens, his energy lifts, and it's more like a lily floating on a pond than a lemon going thru a tube of toothpaste. He floats, his energy is relaxed and his body is loose and fluid. He becomes almost angelic.

I share this story not to invalidate his call to the drum in any way, as it's worthy to recognize the dedication he has to working thru his discomforts there. He uses the drum to help him with some deeper internal stresses and the drum is more of his sort of "not fun" therapy (though he does enjoy it and have fun too) that he feels he needs to do. There is so much value in working in the areas where we know we're uncomfortable and being dedicated to mastering those parts of ourselves, and on an artistic level there is much to be said about finding and riding our edges. My point in this sharing is simply to bring attention to another tool for empowering the beginning steps of your journey, which is to start with your most natural expression, and let your Muse unfold from that place. That may not be your most challenging or fullest expression. It may not even be the place that it will carry you eventually to find within yourself, but if you start there and trust your process, it will guide you to the depths of your being.

For me, I started dancing before I drummed, because dancing was natural and accessible. I understood it in my body, I had access to it regularly, and when I went to drumming, it was an instant and effortless transmission of what my body already knew into my hands. Once I started to drum, my voice came next, then words in rhythm, then more melodies, and more complex combinations of it! Our bodies have deep innate wisdom, and if we just let them lead us, there is no limit to what we can experience. Starting with something that is accessible and natural is the obvious and most effortless entry way and will allow you space for the what next in time! Just because you started crawling first, never meant that you wouldn't walk, and walking never stopped you from being able to swim, run, dance or play hockey. Again, small consistent steps that are not intimidating will bring you towards your Muse and invite it to play with you without scaring it back into it's lonely little shell beneath your skin!

So, maybe now you're thinking to yourself: "Great, but how do I find what's natural for me?" It may sound absurd to you now, but the truth is: you already know, or your body does. There is an innate wisdom in the body that will show you and teach you. If you take some time to observe, listen, feel and allow the transmission of information between your mind and your body to surface you will find that it speaks through you all the time in sometimes subtle, and sometimes obvious ways!

To start with, watch yourself when music is happening around you. Listen *inside*, with more than your physical sense of hearing, and take note of what is happening! When you listen to music, what happens first? Do your hands start moving on your legs tapping out the pulse? Do your fingers tap? Do your feet start moving or wanting to tap or move to the beat? Do your hips start to sway first, or do you want to belt out the melody line and sing at the top of your lungs? Do you sing in the shower or in the car when no one else is around and find it liberating? Is the chorus the height of the music for you?

Put on some of your favorite music right now and listen, but with more than your ears, listen with your whole being engaged in the process. This is the "active" listening I talked about earlier in the book that music making will teach you. Active listening, over time, allows you to drop in to instantly as you practice it more and more. Notice what you connect with first. Maybe you'll want to listen to a few different kinds of music and see if there is variance in how your body responds. Maybe jazz makes you want to tap your fingers, but soul makes you want to sing. Drum music makes you want to dance, and strings just don't do it for you at all, but wow, the accordian really gets you grooving. Maybe you hear words, and get your own little doo-whops going in the background, creating your own vocal parts out of a song, like I did for years before I started to sing and write lyrics.

Remember, there's no part that is more or less important than another! Music needs all aspects of expression it to be complete, so don't judge your own unique expression in any way or on any level! Your natural connection may just be one that isn't well represented in music yet and you may be contributing something totally new and fresh, so let it all come forth! Some of the greatest artists and musicians were daring enough to validate their own expression and put it out there in spite of what was popular, "acceptable" or even in existance, and it was indeed their uniqueness that made them famous and great! So never discount your own unique, whacky, wild or even seemingly absurd creative voice! You never know who and/or what you may inspire!

Finding what's natural for you is a great way to introduce yourself to your authentic and natural potentials and affinities in music. Starting there allows you a place to explore from. Once you have an idea of what you are naturally inclined and drawn to, you can explore all other possibilities in relation to that natural connection and then find your edges to push and grow into. Keep your mind open too! Just because you played guitar 15 years ago, or 2 years ago, doesn't mean that you are going to be naturally drawn to that expression now. We change and evolve thru our lives, and you may find that if you're really paying attention, the guitar just isn't what's calling you now and inside there is a new mystery ready to be unveiled. If you follow what's coming naturally, you can tap into unimaginable possibilities! Trust your body and it's intuitive wisdom and allow yourself time to unveil your Muse. See it as a playful process, an exploration of your self and enjoy every piece that comes forth for what it offers you!

Respecting Your Process: Be Patient and Persevere

The Modern world teaches us "Instant Gratification:" that we can have it all, and we can have it NOW. The whole concept of a "Process" has become, for many, too much to bear, a "pain" in the you know what. Many people feel they just don't have time or energy for it in our rush rush, "get it done now" worlds. We've been effectively trained out of "taking time" by everything from fast food to the web to instant access mentalities. I have a dear friend who comes to mind, one of my closest friends. He just has such an aversion to the concept of "process." The moment a discussion even tries to begin, he just tunes out, energetically abandons the situation, and his reply to being called on it is always the same, "I'm just not into Processing." It's always made me a little confused, as for me "process" brings understanding and ultimately liberation. A process is defined as "a series of natural occurrences that produce change or development!" For me, this represents infinite possibilities, but for the mind affected by Modern Culture, the over stimulated, depressed or exhausted mind, or the mind trained into "Instant Gratification" the idea of a process just seems like too much to bear, too tedious and too lengthy.

There is such joy in any process if we surrender to it and acknowledge the wisdom that comes from it! There's no need to be afraid of it, run from it, or be "too tired" to deal with it. What really makes us tired is the stimulus that creates the need for change! The processing itself is the release of that energy and the shift into a new possibility or a new way of being. Somehow we can often create this heaviness around processing that denies us the joy of discovery and the magic of exploring possibility! Imagine if any of the great explorers of our time had just given up. "Electricity, aah, we know it's out there, it's too much work to figure it out, forget about it! I'm too tired to go through the experiments." "Sure we could make a vehicle that would fly across the oceans, but *man* would that be a process! I'm just not into processing all that data!" It's ridiculous to consider, but in some ways that's what modern life is teaching us. If it's too much work, if we actually have to go thru a series of natural occurrences to get something done, then it's too much bother, so don't bother. If it's too hard, then we can't. If it takes more than 10 minutes to "deal" with it, that's just too long. If you look at the messages that we get on a daily basis you can find many examples of how Modern Culture is reinforcing this behavior and aversion to following through with a process!

Just as life itself is indeed a process, unveiling your Authentic Inner Muse is a process. It can happen in a minute, and yet it can also take months and years to fully reveal itself through you. It may start in one expression and move and dance thru you in many forms until you find your fullest and most empowered voice, be it on the drum, a flute, guitar or some combination of the Muses. Staying present to the unfolding, listening with deep wisdom, and moving thru any challenges or "blocks" that come up with perseverance, compassion and patience creates a constant invitation to your own spirit to continue it's journey, and for the Muses to continue to awaken in you in new and unexpected ways. Patience is a virture, and perseverance is a must if we are to live as fully expressed and complete beings. Again, the example this sets for others in our lives provides such a needed model for the human race. When we become more empowerd in our expressions, we invite and allow others to do the same. So know that by you doing your part to find your own voice, you are also contributing to the empowerment of others to find theirs. Keep on keeping on, don't judge yourself, and whatever you do: don't give up on yourself!

Creating a New Groove:
Reprogramming the "I Can't" with "Yes I can"

If we think of our mental processes like grooves, like a rhythm track that just keeps on running through our minds, we can create a musical metaphor to play with the idea of reprogramming our thoughts around music making, or really around anything in our lives. If you want to start making music, make a new groove to replace the old one that has been telling you you can't or you're not good enough, or you don't know how, or you're too old, whatever it is for you. To do that, and in essence to make any groove, you first have to establish some kind of solid foundation. It's not as hard as it may seem. The foundation, in essence, is simply your own desire to bring music into your life!

"Your desire to Muse is the desire you must use!" Your desire has to be strong enough to outwit your mind! You'll need to be vigilant and watch your thoughts and reactions like you would a 2 year old. You'll need to summon up your sense of humor and a good dose of compassion with yourself to move fully thru this one, but have no doubt: you can do it! It doesn't matter what your "old" programming, or "story" says anymore, because you are now choosing to create a new one. This is also a great exercise in disciplining the mind and can be applied to all aspects of our lives. Always our minds want to try to dictate what "is" and "is not." In order to create effective and long lasting change, we have to create a relationship between our "will" and our "mind" so that they work together to co-create the new pattern.

It's kind of like disciplining a young child who loves to play in kitchen garbage. Every time they go to the garbage, you gently move them from it to something else, say a doll or a bag of toys that is far from the kitchen garbage can. They play with it for a minute, put it down, and go back to the garbage, pulling an egg shell out with glee and rubbing it all over their face. And so, you go back to the child, lovingly, laughing and move it back to the bag of toys, firmly saying, "No" to the garbage and wiping the goop off the face and handing the child the more suitable and healthier toy. There is no need to slap the child or scream and berate it when it goes to the garbage, it just doesn't know better yet and it hasn't created the "groove" for the desired behavior yet! Again and again this cycle will repeat, until eventually the child is covered in garbage happily playing with their doll or toy in the middle of the living room. The garbage now a faint smell lingering from an old meal. The positive reinforcement of the new behavior has created lasting and permanent change in the "groove" of the mind and the child has learned that there are better things to do than play in garbage and more suitable toys than egg shells.

We have to be vigilant, loving and firm with our minds. They can keep us stuck for lifetimes in stinky rotting garbage, repeating the same toxic thought patterns over and over and then creating ways that those patterns become reinforced and supported in our lives daily. It's a cycle that takes attention and discipline to break and then re-program with what we really want from/in ourselves. The mind is often compared to a child (and sometimes a monkey) and it is a great metaphor: always active, always needing discipline that is loving, joyful and compassionate, always needing to be watched. It's important not to beat ourselves up, or be cruel to ourselves when we find ourselves again playing in the garbage of our minds. Instead, if we want lasting change, we must lovingly remember there are better options than self destructive talk or thoughts, and return again and again to the new program, the desired action. When we give the mind a new possibility and something new to entertain itself with, eventually, the new thought begins to replace the old and the old will be forgotten as the new groove is created and reinforced!

Overcoming Fear of Inadequacy: Stop Judging Already!

The fear of inadequacy, or unworthiness, lives in almost all of us at some time or another in some way. Inadequacy is defined as the failure to reach a required or expected standard. When we can really honor our humanness and have compassion for that place in ourselves and others, we get to move from it into recognizing the journey from there is upward and onward. All of the above mentioned concepts in this chapter can help you to conquer this fear effectively. In addition, consider this: if we hold no expectation on ourselves for any certain standard in our musical experiences, but are really honoring just the experience itself, in and of itself, then suddenly there is no judging, no "standard" to live up to anymore! So, how is it then possible to be inadequate?

Take away the expectation of how you think it should look or feel, and just be present to what is without deeming it "good" or "bad." Your expression is your expression. How can you possibly put a label on it or compare it to anyone else's in the world? It's absurd, it's like comparing a butterfly to a cucumber. Each individual is so unique, with such different life experiences that make up their form of expression. It is simply unfair to compare ourselves to anyone or anything else or to judge ourselves accordingly.

Some of the most amazing things happen when we stop trying to direct the outcome and stop judging ourselves or our creations as "good enough," "better than" or "not as good as." There is no competition, no need to prove anything to anyone. There is no need to act like, be like or sound like anything other than what we really are. You are enough and you are complete within yourself! I know our culture doesn't reinforce this everywhere, but that doesn't mean we have to continue to subscribe to some sick illusion that we're never quite good enough, never quite there, never quite as cool as so and so, because we don't have such and such. What a nightmarish concept of insanity! Keeping up with the Jones to the umpteenth degree has made us a society of neurotic basket cases feeling always like we've got to have the latest, newest, freshest car or gadget, be informed of every world situation, know the latest and always have our fingers on the pulse in every way.

We don't have to "keep up" with any one else, or feel like because we don't that we're less! That goes especially for the creative arts and for our basic human experiences, relationships and in building communities! Being yourself is enough and however that comes thru you musically and creatively is perfect!

If you want to start to bring the Music out of yourself, don't judge it or yourself. Don't even begin to think "Oh, I don't sound as pretty as she does," or "I'm not as groovy as him." One: it's probably not true, and two: you're not them! You'll never sound the same as anyone else if you're being 100% authentic! Your rhythm will always be a little different than anyone else's as will your voice! Your life experiences are different and unique and so your expressions will, of course, be unique.

Imitation is not authenticity! You can learn someone else's music and maybe even sound like them, but if that's all you ever do, then sad to say, you've never found your true authentic self or your own creativity and you've never really allowed for truly Authentic Musing!

Music is simply for the joy of the expression. It's a place of purity. The fear of being not good enough is a product of Western thought, the glamorization of music, and modern culture. Traditional peoples and folk music invite everyone: there's no standard to judge by, no "perfect" voice or "best" player. Everyone has a voice, so everyone sings, in their own way. Everyone who can dance, dances, it's not all about who dances better or who's sexier. It's about being together, sharing the human experience and being alive. Sharing music is about honoring all voices equally and with reverence.

Again, if you're looking to be a classical master, at some point you'll likely be considering your technical proficiencies and skills, which ones need work, which ones you've mastered, etc. There is a different set of priorities for a musician choosing that path and some "imitation" may be necessary for them in their career to demonstrate certain skills, or to make money in their profession. There is a huge distinction in that path than the one I'm discussing which is just getting you to play some music! Gettiing you past the programming that has been holding you back from your Muses to a place where you can feel empowered in your authentic, natural expression! Once the Muses have awakened in you, there is no telling where you'll go!

Life as Music: It's a Way of Life

For many people, finding a place to just be able to be quiet can be very difficult, much less finding a place to sing, dance and be Museful or practice and develop a new emerging Muse. Utilize what you have. Don't wait until you have the "perfect" situation to start finding and getting acquainted with your Muses. If you have a commute, use your drive time to sing or practice your active listening skills. Next time it rains when you're driving, listen for the rhythm of your windshield wipers and sing to that! I do it all the time, it's super fun! When no one else is in the car it's a perfect time for you to play, explore, and get silly with yourself. I have a little diddy I sing sometimes in the Muse and in my shows to encourage people to sing: "Don't really matter what you say, just open your mouth let your spirit play." Just sing! Sing to the car next to you, sing your trip, sing what you're feeling, seeing, and experiencing. Have you noticed that the songs that touch you inside are experiences that you relate to? Sing your heart song, and again, judge not! Your song is your song, no one else can ever sing it the way you will!

Another tool for your tool box is to become more conscious of rhythms around you.   Open your perceptive abilities and use your down time waiting in line or in traffic, or at the Dr. office as an exercise in Active Musical Listening and participation.   See what you can or do "entrain" (or sync in) with naturally, in your environment. Listen for melodies, harmonies, overtones, and sing what inspires you the most. You can even sing in your head if your somewhere you can't sing out loud. If you ride a bus or a train, feel the grooves of the wheels beneath you, notice the rhythm of the ride you're on, tap it out on your leg.   You don't have to have an instrument. *You are the instrument.* It's a much more constructive use of your time than what your mind might typically be doing.   Think about it: what else would you be doing mentally? Running that old familiar programming in your mind probably: convincing yourself you don't have time to become more musical, you've got too much to do: did you water the plants last week, why did Joe talk to me that way yesterday, I'm so sick of my job, blah blah blah.   Meanwhile, that whole 20 minutes is gone. Time that could have been used as reflective time to listen to your inner Muses and the Muses of Life was wasted in the overactive mind's attachments to the non-relative past. That time was wasted in thoughts that stressed you out, brought you down and kept you stuck in the same old same old self defeating paradigm.   All that time, you could have been experiencing the Music of Life of the present and playing *with creation* rather than stuck in the stagnancy of the mind.

Dance in your kitchen with your kids, or your partner or friends, while you're making dinner.   A twirl here, a hip swing there, and voila Veggie Burgers ala boogie down funkadelic!   And a very fun mom or dad with some happy laughing kids, who may indeed think you've gone kooky, but so what! Even better you are now modeling for those around you that life can be fun, joyful and playful rather than offering yet another example of the "adult" paradigm that being "grown up" means no more fun.   You might find it contagious and in the arms of your partner suddenly swooned! And if you don't, and you instead get the grump treatment, don't let that discourage you or shut you down for another year or even a day! Have compassion and respect for your partner's choice to stay grumpy, and use it as fuel in a loving way of course! Affirm that you want to keep the Muse alive, in your head, in your body, in your spirit so that you don't catch the grump bug which can also be contagious at times! Keep your Muse going inside: it will keep you alive if you keep it alive!

Music is more than just an obscure art form. Music is a way of life. It is a way of living that allows for more of ourselves than what we can see. Consider all the aspects of the Muses: the music, the dance, the poetry, the rhythm, the melody, the emotional content, and see if you can find some place for at least one piece of it every day in your life. Maybe Monday you sing in the shower, Tuesday you take a dance class, Wednesday you listen to something you really love, Thursday you just listen to the Rhythms of Life, and on the weekend you go to see a concert or find a local community music jam. In this way you are building the Muse into your life as *a way of life*. As you bring the Muse into your life more and more, you will start to see it showing up more and more around you and more effortlessly thru you. It will naturally begin unveiling itself in the most unexpected places and ways, and in time you will become the Muse itself, expressed in a unique and beautiful way that only you can share with the world!

Bringing The Muse into your Community

"At the moment when we really do need to reinvent the wheels, the traditions, the ways of music making, we discover how little we know about what makes these wheels turn and keep on turning. Surely there is lots of research to do, but it is not so much on others, it is on us. And it is urgent. (Keil)"

We were not born in little bubbles. We were not designed to live isolated and alone. Humans are a social species by nature's design. We thrive when we live, work, play and share together, and die when we are isolated too much. We must experiment, explore and play *together* to learn how to be in relationships that foster well-being, long lasting friendships and mutual respect. We have been given the capacity to love, nurture, share and co-exist. In many cultures of the world this is the norm. Somewhere the idealogy of this nation has turned itself into a big lonely depressed mass of fearful, isolated beings crying in their own hearts for some way to be connected. All of the symptoms discussed in chapter 1 have some relationship to this issue. Sociologists are gravely concerned for the future of western society and the individuals in it because of the increasing levels of isolationism, and the resultant depression, crime, suicide and other social problems it spawns. We need models to work with to provide people the opportunity to reach out and learn to work and play together again. We need to experiment together to find the models that work.

Community Music is one model that has been proven to be effective in helping to bring people together to heal, transform and shift consciousness and to provide therapeutic effects to body, mind and spirit. Making music gets sweeter, and more profound the more it is shared and explored with others. Once you start to feel it in your own life, you will naturally want to find others to play with, share with and create with! The Muse has an innate contagious, playful spirit that yearns for shared creative play and expression. Finding playmates may not be as hard as you might think at first.

You may find that there is already something happening in your town that you can plug into to begin with. Look around for drum circles, or community dances and see what's already happening close to home. Check your daily papers, online, and in the local arts/music publications. If those groups do exist they can be a great place to find people who may be interested in something new and/or exploring other possibilities. Or it may be simply a place you can begin to share with others on a regular basis! You can host a gathering at your home, or find a community space to use: yoga centers, community centers, recreation centers and even garages can be great places to bring people together and many centers are often very excited to offer something of this nature!

Keep in mind all of the pieces of this chapter in relationship to building a group. Don't set yourself, or your group, up for failure, find what's natural, etc. All of these tools I've offered will apply to the group process just as they do for the individual's process. Group dynamics are a fascinating study and a wonderful opportunity for personal reflection. In taking any initiative to help bring people together to share, you are offering a beautiful service and a gift to your community that will blossom in your life in many unforetold ways throughout your life. You may also find many unique challenges, joys and experiences that expand you in multi-dimensional facets of your being! Remaining humble, staying consistent and being willing to learn and grow with your group will bring you years of unimaginable magic and personal growth. It also will foster a community that will strengthen over time as it learns how to communicate and share, dance and sing, ebb and flow and the relationships will flourish far beyond just the Music. The music will be the catalyst, but what follows extends far beyond it into life long learnings!

If you want to start a group, and feel you need help, you can always contact me, or other Community Music Making specialists to help you. I am always excited to help spread the love and joy of community music making and will do everything I can to help you get started. You can contact me through my web site: www.cherishanti.com. I feel I speak for most of us who know the beauty and power of this work: we are more than happy to help you along your way. It is our service and joy to spread this to the world!

Conclusion:

Finding your own musical expression is one of the most joyful and rewarding things you can do for yourself. Music is one activity that can be enjoyed literally for a whole lifetime, from childhood to old age. Music heals, transforms and creates balance in our lives in a very unique way that is still revealing itself! Research continues to provide us insights into the why's and how's of it all from neurology to biology, physiology and more. For me, with or without the science to prove it, I just know that when I'm in the groove, I'm home. I feel complete, whole, and expanded.

I sincerely hope that you will cultivate time and appreciation in your life to explore your inner self thru music and the Muse of your own being!

I welcome your stories, comments and sharings in any form on my blog: www.muselove.blogspot.com or to me personally thru my web site.

Remember: Sharing is the gift you give to others and when you help to empower another to find their own song or dance, you are changing their world and the world around us all!

Works Cited

Aboriginal Art. <http://www.aboriginalart.com>.

Altonn, Helen. "Music Helps Reduce Stress." Honolulu Star Bulletin 29 Apr. 2004.

"A big YES for Music." Diss. Music Educators National Conference, 1997. Abstract.

"Breathing Space." Breathing Space. Breathing Space. <http://www. breathingspacescotland.co.uk>.

Capoeira, Nestor. "Roots of the Dance-Fight Game." Wikkipedia. Jan. 2008 <http://wikkipedia.org>.

Cheater, Angela P., ed. The Anthropology of Power : Empowerment and Disempowerment in Changing Structures. New York: Routledge, 1999.

Dangerous Decibels. <http://www.dangerousdecibels.org>.

Dissanayake, Ellen. "Ritual and Ritualization." Music and Manipulation on the Social Control of Music. New York: Berghahn Books, Incorporated, 2006.

Farmelo, Allen. "The Unifying Aspects of Grooving: An Introductory Ethnographic Approach thru Music." (1997).

FDA. <http://www.fda.gov>.

Fenton, Ben. "Junk Culture is Poisoning our Children." Telegraph News. 13 Sept. 2006.Telegraph News.<http:///www.telegraph.co.uk/ news>.

Future of Music Coalition. Future of Music Coalition. Jan. 2008 <http://www.futureofmusic.org>.

Garcia, Antonio. "The Necessity of Music Education." Feb. 2008 <http://www.garciamusic.com>.

Heth, Charlotte. "Overview." The Garland Encyclopedia of World Music. 367-68.

Kammen, Carole, and Jodi Gold. Call to Connection : Bringing
Sacred Tribal Values into Modern Life. Grand Rapids: Commune-A-
Key, Incorporated, 1998.

Keil, Charles. "Muse Incorporating and Applied Sociomusicology."
Muse Kids. Feb. 2008 <http://www.musekids.org>.

Khan, Anahat I. The Music of Life. Minneapolis: Omega
Publications, Incorporated, 1998.

Lachance, Kim. "Even Toddlers Get the Blues." Psych Central. 10
Dec. 2006. Jan. 2008 <http://psychcentral.com>.

Levitin, Daniel J. This Is Your Brain on Music : The Science of a
Human Obsession. New York: Plume, 2007.

Lewis, Catherine, and Ineko Tsuchida. "What's Basic in Japan?"

Milun, Kathryn. "Rock Music and National Identity in Hungary." 26
July 2003. Free Republic. Jan.-Feb. 2008 <http://www.freerepublic.
com>.

Marcus, George E., ed. Perilous States : Conversations on Culture,
Politics, and Nation. New York: University of Chicago P, 1994.

Murray, Ian. "Clubbers Risk Losing the Sound of Silence." The
Deafened People Page. 3 Aug. 1999. Deafened. <http://www.
deafened.org/>.

"Music Making." American Music Conference. American Music
Conference. <http://www.amc-music.com/>.

O'Neill, Dr Susan. "Understanding the Decline in Children's Music
Participation following the Transition to Secondary School." Dept of
Psychology, Keele University.

Orford, Emily-Jane. "A Place for Music: The importance of Music
Education in The Public School System." Fermata (University of
Victoria) (2001).

"Prehistoric Music/Folk Music/Tribal Music." Music: Folk, Prehistoric, Modern, More. Wikkopedia. <http://en.wikipedia.org/>.

Rietveld, Hillegonda C. "The Body and Soul of Club Culture."

Unesco. Jan.-Feb. 2008 <http://www.unesco.org>.

Royal Institute for Deaf People. <http://www.rnid.org.uk>.

Sairam, TV _. "Indian Music and it's Aesthetic Concepts." World Music Central. 3 Oct. 2007. World Music Central. Jan. 2008 <http:// worldmusiccentral.org>.

Sallie Bingham Center. Duke University. <http://library.duke.edu>.

School Music Matters. <http://www.schoolmusicmatters.com>.

Seargant, Jack. "Sonic Weapons." Fortean Times. <http://www. forteantimes.com/features/articles/256/sonic_weapons.html>.

Small, Chris. "Musicking: A Ritual in Social Space."

Sokolova, Irina V. "Depression in Children: What Causes it and how can we help." Rochester Institute of Technology. Jan. 2008 <http:// www.personalityresearch.org>.

"The Sound of Silence: The Unprecedented Decline of Music Education in California Schools." Music for All. Sept. 2004. Music for All. Feb. 2008 <http://www.music-for-all.org>.

Walker, Sheila S. African Roots - American Cultures : Africa in the Creation of the Americas. New York: Rowman and Littlefield, Incorporated, 2001.

Wallaschek, Richard. Primitive Music: An Inquiry into the Origin and Devlopment of Music, Songs, Instruments, Dances and Pantomines of Savage Races. London: Longmans Green, 1893.

Wallin, Nils L., Bj Merker, and Steven Brown, eds. The Origins of Music. New York: MIT P, 2001.

"What is Folk Music." School of Information. University of Michigan. Jan. 2008 <http://www.si.umich.edu/chico/folkandblues/music_folk.htm>.

"World Problems/Social Issues." Union of International Associates. Union of International Associates. <http://www.diversitas.org>.

Writer, Sport. "Fairfax County Schools Struggle with Cuts Across the Board." Associated Content Jan. 2008. Associated Content. 21 Jan. 2008. Feb. 2008 <http://www.associatedcontent.com>.

Made in the USA
Lexington, KY
12 August 2014